"SEX has emerged in our times as something used to sell cigarettes, automobiles, and jeans; to measure personal appeal; to rate in films. It is something you 'have' with somebody. It is an alien entity now spreading more and more widely through our culture, becoming ever more trivial and impersonal. And yet, the 'sex' that dominates our days and nights is by no means *real*. It does not exist in nature but is, rather, an idea, an abstraction, a construct of the human mind. . . . Something called 'human sexuality' would have been meaningless to Dante, Shakespeare, or Goethe. 'Sex,' in short, is an idea whose time has passed."

from THE END OF SEX

"Sexual liberation . . . frees the individual not only from inhibition but also from commitment, yet erotic love demands commitment. Through narrative, memoir, and social analysis, Leonard reinterprets the meaning of intimacy and provides readers with some deeply felt insights."

—*Booklist*

"Long overdue. . . . What it says needs to be said."

—*Booksellers*

"Compelling."

—*Mademoiselle*

BANTAM NEW AGE BOOKS

This important new imprint includes books in a variety of fields and disciplines and deals with the search for meaning, growth and change. BANTAM NEW AGE BOOKS form connecting patterns to help understand this search as well as mankind's options and models for tomorrow. They are books that circumscribe our times and our future.

The End of Sex

*Erotic Love After
the Sexual Revolution*

George Leonard

BANTAM BOOKS
TORONTO · NEW YORK · LONDON · SYDNEY

THE END OF SEX
*A Bantam Book / published by arrangement with
J. P. Tarcher, Inc.*

PRINTING HISTORY
*J. P. Tarcher edition published January 1983
Serlialized in Reader's Digest, March 1983; Cosmopolitan,
Fall 1983 and Los Angeles Times Syndicate.*

Bantam edition / March 1984

*The author would like to thank the following for permission to
reprint:*

*Harold Robbins, The Betsy. Copyright © 1971 by Harold Robbins.
Reprinted by permission of Simon & Schuster, a Division of Gulf &
Western Corporation.*

*Norman Mailer, Advertisements for Myself. Reprinted by permis-
sion of the author and the author's agents, Scott Meredith Literary
Agency, Inc., 845 Third Avenue, New York, 10022.*

*Excerpt Delta of Venus: Erotica by Anaïs Nin, Copyright © 1969
Anaïs Nin Trust. Reprinted by permission of Harcourt Brace
Jovanovich, Inc.*

*From Portrait of the Artist as a Young Man by James Joyce.
Copyright © 1916 by D. W. Huebsch. Copyright © 1944 by Nora
Joyce. Definitive text Copyright © 1964 by the Estate of James
Joyce. Reprinted by permission of Viking Penguin, Inc.*

*New Age and the accompanying figure design as well as the
statement "a search for meaning, growth and change" are trade-
marks of Bantam Books, Inc.*

ISBN 0-553-23927-9

For Annie Styron Leonard
With whom dream and reality have at last joined
Through whom I have experienced lasting love
Without whom this book could never have been written

Acknowledgments

ONCE AGAIN, as in my previous five books, I want to express my deep gratitude to Leo Litwak, who suggested that I address the subject of erotic love. I thank him for his continuing encouragement and guidance, and for enlightening conversations during hundreds of miles of running together.

John and Julia Poppy have been instrumental in making this book a reality. They are part of it, and of my life, in more ways than one.

I have been especially fortunate during this project to have had the advocacy and counsel of my four daughters, Ellen Burr Leonard, Mimi Leonard Rubin, Lillie Pitts Leonard II, and Emily Winship Leonard.

For informed and most helpful readings, I thank Richard Cowan, Dr. John R. Lee, Drs. John and Judith Luce, Joan A. Nelson, Jerry Rubin, Saul-Paul Sirag, and Keith Thompson.

My warm appreciation goes again to Sterling Lord for his firm support and friendship.

A very special acknowledgment must be made here to Millie Loeb and Jeremy Tarcher. In their joint editorship, they have given me the challenge, guidance, and nurture that I once believed had gone out of style in the publishing "industry." Their patience, energy, intelligence, and concern should stand as a beacon for all who care about books.

And, finally, there are the scores of people that I have interviewed on erotic love over the past four years. As it has turned out, I have used only a few of the interviews verbatim, but all have inspired and informed me and led me to admire the ingenuity, courage, and humor of ordinary people in dealing with "sex" in extraordinary times. More than anything else, those wonderfully candid and often intense talks have confirmed for me the enduring desire—even in an age of recreational sex—for passionate, fully committed love.

Contents

Beyond the Sexual Revolution

LIKE MILLIONS of other Americans, I welcomed the Sexual Revolution of the 1960s. I even did my own small part, through books, articles, and special issues of *Look*, to help it along. How healthy this Revolution seemed! After years—centuries—of repression, we were now to be free to discuss sexual matters in mixed company, to live together openly without being married, to enjoy our own sexual preferences without fear of prejudice, to obtain sexual information and birth control devices easily, to see erotic films and read erotic books, to try out previously forbidden acts and share erotic fantasies with our mates.

The Revolution enjoyed one swift victory after another. Filmed and printed erotica that would have shocked in 1965 brought yawns in 1975. Within less than a decade, the sexual experiments of East and West Coast college students and hippies became the common practices of blue collar workers in Des Moines and Texarkana. Perhaps never before had such a radical shift in mores occurred in so short a time. Surely we were on our way to an erotic utopia, a society in which informed, mutually consenting individuals could fully realize themselves sexually without public opprobrium or personal guilt.

Not quite.

The sheer speed and scope of the change have produced a highly visible backlash. Well-financed lobby groups of the Moral Right, along with allies in all three branches of government, are now working impatiently to reverse the Sexual Revolution and return the nation to what they call "family values." The vehemence of the Moral Right has produced dismay among sexual reformers, who, pointing to the persistence of sexual ignorance, prejudice, fear, and guilt, believe that the Revolution has not gone nearly far enough.

But the Moral Right, despite its visibility, probably represents the views of no more than a fourth of the population.[1] The great majority of Americans favor sex education in the schools and oppose making abortion illegal, just to mention two hotly contested issues.[2] Gratefully, if quietly, most people in the United States and many other advanced industrial nations support the aims and gains of the Sexual Revolution. Given the sleazy and exploitative nature of some of the products of the Revolution, I can well understand the outrage of the attackers. I also sympathize with all reasonable efforts to strengthen the family. But I do not support the aims or the methods of the Moral Right, and I suspect that in the long run its attacks will fail.

Biology has been considerably more effective than the Moral Right in dampening hopes for a utopia of free love. The recent spread of genital herpes has had an especially chilling effect on those engaged in the sport of sexual conquest. These biological developments, however, are receiving wide attention in the news media and in other books, and will not be discussed here.

For me, the truly fundamental problem lies neither in biology nor the backlash but in the structure of the reform movement itself. For the Sexual Revolution, in slaying some loathsome old dragons, has brought to light some formidable new ones. Victorian proscription has been replaced by subtle but pervasive prescription. The terrifying injunctions against masturbation, for example, have yielded to the sexological counsel that masturbation is good for you: as therapy, self-realization, political statement, *duty*. Humane assumptions of the Revolution, unquestioned and unchallenged, have become ideology, which has become dogma: That immediate pleasure and satisfaction are the chief aims of sexual activity. That the application of knowledge through technique is the best way of getting pleasure and satisfaction. That "sex problems" can be specified and matched with specific solutions, which require expert advice and/or treatment. That an active, varied, and intense sex life is an unqualified good, a goal to be pursued by every human being, regardless of gender, age, or physical condition. "Old-fashioned religious moralism," says philosopher Sam Keen, "was permissive indeed compared to our hip erotic methodism."

Looming over all of this, puffed up to enormous dimensions, is something called "sex"—an activity, a field of study, an entity that somehow seems to exist almost entirely separated from the rest of life. In the minds and practices of the reformers, sex has long been separated from love; you can read scores of current sex books and never once come across the word "love." To take one case, the three separate questionnaires used for *The Hite Report* contained a total of 173 questions, only two of which touched upon love. Question 58 in the first questionnaire asked women to free-associate sex with childbearing, going to the bathroom, pleasure, love, or "other." The second questionnaire failed to mention love. Question 33 in the third questionnaire placed the word "love" in quotes and reflected, through considerable grammatical and semantic confusion, a certain queasiness about having brought the subject up:

33. If you have ever experienced something you called "love," which emotions were involved? Was it, or were they, a healthy or unhealthy relationship? How did these relationships affect sex?[3]

11

Sex has also been divorced from creation. I've come across only one recent book in the area of sexuality, June Singer's *Androgyny*, that mentions creation or the creative process. Singer shows that ancient and primitive cultures saw a close relationship between the act of love and the process of creation—not just of babies, but of matter, earth, sky, water, islands, monsters, and gods. We seem to have simply forgotten this ancient connection.

What's more, the majority of sex books never even mention *pro*creation, which might lead one to think that we of the late twentieth century, like our earliest ancestors, are unaware that sexual intercourse has anything to do with the subsequent birth of a child. The Sexual Revolution is indeed shot through with paradoxes. We are led to believe, for example, that sex is a natural, healthy function, an enjoyment of daily life. At the same time, we are permitted to disconnect it from most social and ethical considerations. This disconnection makes us think that our erotic behavior actually has little to do with anything else that we believe, feel, or do, and is thus essentially trivial.

Sex has emerged, then, in our times as something used to sell cigarettes, automobiles, and jeans; to measure personal appeal; to rate in films. It is something you "have" with somebody. It is an alien entity now spreading more and more widely through our culture, becoming ever more trivial and impersonal. And yet, the "sex" that dominates our days and nights is by no means *real*. It does not exist in nature but is, rather, an idea, an abstraction, a construct of the human mind. Even the word itself in most of its current usages and combinations (see Chapter Eight) is of a fairly recent origin. Something called "human sexuality" would have been meaningless to Dante, Shakespeare, or Goethe.

"Sex," in short, is an idea whose time has passed. It might have been useful in defining a field of study and focusing attention on certain modern problems, but it has outgrown its usefulness as a concept. It is by no means needed for understanding and expressing the varieties of erotic feeling and action. It has become, in fact, an enemy to the realization of erotic love.

Already, we are seeing a growing resistance to "sex" and all that it implies, not among members of the Moral Right, but among those most deeply involved in the Sexual Revolution. A September 1980 *Cosmopolitan* magazine sex survey of more than 106,000 women, for example, confirmed that a Revolution has indeed taken place in sexual behavior as well as attitude. But it also showed that a majority of the women surveyed were disillusioned and disappointed with "the emotional fruit the sex revolution has borne." According to the *Cosmopolitan* report, "So many readers wrote negatively about the sexual revolution, expressing longings for vanished intimacy, and the now elusive joys of romance and commitment, that we began to sense that there might be a sexual counterrevolution underway in America."

But would a counterrevolution be enough? Revolution is literally a turn of the wheel; what was on top ends up at the bottom and vice versa. It seems to me that we need something *beyond* the Sexual Revolution, beginning with a new way of perceiving and conceptualizing the erotic realm, not another turn of the wheel of repression and liberation. This does not require renouncing the humane reforms that have come out of the Sexual Revolution, but, rather, those reforms need to be put into a new context.

For a start, I think we need to discard the entire idea encoded in the present usage of the word "sex," along with the dangerous trivialization, fragmentation, and depersonalization of life that it encourages. We need to reconnect the bedroom with the rest of our lives, with society, and nature, and perhaps with the stars. We need to realize that the way we make love influences the way we make our world, and vice versa. We need to appreciate the connection between the erotic and the creative. We need, more than anything else, to reawaken to the almost-endless, half-forgotten, life-transforming powers of full-bodied, fully committed erotic love.

This book is offered as a preview of and a guide to the

end of "sex" and the renewal of erotic love. It is not a how-to book. One of my main theses, in fact, is that specific techniques and sets of instructions are useless and even counterproductive in the realm of the erotic. I offer not instructions but perceptions, thoughts, and feelings, in the belief that the way we perceive, think, and feel must eventually change our experience and our actions. My hope is that the reader will find making love somehow different after reading the following chapters.

The End of Sex is not a formal, step-by-step argument for a specific proposition or point of view, but rather it is a combination of varied elements: fiction, memoir, reportage, and essay. Because of this departure from what might be a more familiar format, a brief road map is in order.

Part I—*Love's Power*—begins with a description of the astonishing transformations of the body and the psyche that occur during the act of love. The first chapter is straight exposition. The next two chapters are what I would like to call *informational fiction*. Having an enormous amount of information to convey—on the physiological, endocrinological, neurological, and psychological aspects of the act of love—I determined that the most economical and effective way of presenting it would be in terms of a story. The scientific information in the story has been checked by experts in the fields involved and is, to the best of my knowledge, accurate. As for the human side of this narrative, it is drawn from interviews and talks I have had with scores of people since 1978. But it is primarily a work of the imagination, owing a great deal to my own erotic experience.

In Part II—*Love's Promise*—I present three aspects of my own erotic development, personal material that is included here out of a strong conviction that it is impossible not to do so. I am perhaps belaboring a point to say that every book—even one that strives for total objectivity—is at the deepest level biased. The selection of subject matter and mode of expression, the inclusion or omission of material, the ordering of paragraphs, sentences, and words, the invisible context in which the work exists—all reflect personal experience and express personal bias. In my view, the cleanest way to deal with the inevitable is to present a certain amount of personal revelation explicit. This done, the reader can more readily make adjustments for any personal bias that might be otherwise hidden in seemingly objective presentation.

And to those sex experts who might argue that my ideas represent "merely" my personal erotic predilections, I offer no counter-argument. I do ask, however, that the experts—especially those who have given us the most purportedly objective studies, atlases, and encyclopedias—reveal their own erotic predilections before pursuing any discussion on the subject of objectivity.

Part III—*Eros Betrayed*—starts with a visit to the National Sex Forum, where "sex" holds center stage. While this first chapter is primarily reportage, the four that follow are in essay form. My purpose is to show that while the Sexual Revolution has brought the contradictions in our erotic life into bold relief, these contradictions are deeply imbedded in our culture itself, especially in the matters of abstraction, generalization, and ideology. We abstract and generalize to codify knowledge more effectively, to gain control over nature, and to develop technology. But when we become abstract and general in human affairs, life becomes fragmented and impersonal, and such monstrosities as "sex" are likely to emerge. Ideology can also be useful at times, but it is totally out of place in the erotic realm, where paradox and surprise are the rule. The ravages of abstraction, generalization, and ideology are examined in terms of erotic history, erotic fantasy, views of the person, and views of the body.

The final section, Part IV—*Revisioning the Erotic*—is devoted to a vision of erotic possibilities that lie beyond the end of sex. The first three chapters present the vision in terms of the body, the person and the society. The next two chapters describe the close relationship between the erotic

15

and the creative and show how our perception of this relationship can help transform our erotic experience. The last chapter is an erotic desideratum, a statement of how, if the choice were mine, I would like it to be.

* * *

In the erotic realm, each of us is both an expert and an amateur. We are experts about our own experiences and amateurs about everybody else's. Few things in life are more compelling and conclusive than the inner erotic sense of what feels good and what repels, what is "right" and what is "wrong." My intention in the pages that follow is not to insist that my views are right and others' are wrong, but simply to offer alternative views for your consideration. In doing so, I want to retain my status as an amateur in two senses of the word, as a lover as well as a nonprofessional.

PART I

Love's Power

CHAPTER ONE

The Body Transformed

> The responses which an animal makes when it is stimulated sexually constitute one of the most elaborate and in many respects one of the most remarkable complexes (syndromes) of physiologic phenomena in the whole gamut of mammalian behavior.
>
> —Kinsey, Pomeroy, Martin, and Gebhart,
> *Sexual Behavior in the Human Female*

DURING SEXUAL AROUSAL and consummation, the human body is radically transformed. From head to toe, no cell is entirely unaffected. Sometimes it takes as little as a single word whispered in your lover's ear to trigger this remarkable process. Within seconds, blood starts rushing toward the surface, filling out every distensible area and literally altering your lover's appearance. In the words of Kinsey and his associates:

> The surface outlines of the whole body of one who is sexually aroused become quite different from the outlines of one who is not so aroused. The lobes of the ears may become thickened and swollen. The lips of the mouth may become filled with blood and, in most individuals, more protrudent than under ordinary circumstances. The whole breast, particularly

of the female, may become swollen, enlarged and more protrudent. The anal area may become turgid. The arms and legs may have their outlines altered. The tumescence is so apparent everywhere over the body that it alone is sufficient evidence of the presence of erotic arousal. Women who pretend arousal when there is none may, to some degree, simulate the motions of coitus; but they cannot voluntarily produce the peripheral circulation of blood and the consequent tumescence of the lips, the breasts, the nipples, the labia minora, and the whole body contour which are the unmistakable, and almost invariable evidences of erotic arousal.[1]

This bodily transformation, this look of love, is accompanied by a change in skin coloration. What is known as the sex flush generally begins on the upper abdomen and face. As arousal continues, it moves to the breasts, neck, chest, thighs, arms, lower abdomen, buttocks, and back, deepening in some cases from light to dark red or even to a rich reddish purple. A fine film of perspiration may appear on various parts of the body. The lips become moist and full. The eyes begin to dilate and glisten with increased moisture. As the flesh around the eyes and mouth fills out, facial lines are reduced or erased. The overall effect is a sort of radiance. Years seem to fall away. The middle-aged lover regains the aspect of youth, while the young lover may appear younger yet.

At the same time, the heart begins to beat faster. Pulse rates can increase from a normal 70 a minute to 180 or more at the moment of orgasm. Blood pressure rises dramatically. Diastolic pressures have been known to increase from 65 to 160, and systolic pressures from 120 to 250 or more. Breathing speeds up to the point of hyperventilation, reaching 40 breaths or more a minute. Muscle tone throughout the body increases; the neck becomes rigid; the feet extend and the toes curl; and the fingers may clench and unclench. From head to toe, muscles tense and relax in a steady or convulsive rhythm. Even when there is no external evidence of movement, the entire musculature may begin pulsing slightly during the earliest stages of sexual arousal. As arousal increases, muscular contractions, especially those of the buttocks, pelvis, and thighs, become extremely powerful. Muscular strength is markedly increased, perhaps through the release of inhibition. At the onset of orgasm, you and your lover may resemble Olympic athletes at the peak of the agonistic struggle. Kinsey takes the analogy another step, suggesting that a human individual at the point of sexual climax "presents the traditional aspect of a person being tortured."[2]

There are other startling body changes during the process of erotic arousal—and you might have noted that I haven't yet begun to consider the complex and indeed prodigious behavior of the sexual apparatus during this process. Bleeding from cut blood vessels, for example, may be reduced significantly; strangely enough, that is true even of those bodily parts that are engorged with blood. Hay fever sinus congestion is often relieved. At the same time, the membranes inside the nostrils are likely to secrete more than the usual amounts of mucus. Saliva may be produced in copious amounts. According to Kinsey, "If one's mouth is open when there is a sudden upsurge of erotic stimulation and response, saliva may be spurted some distance out of the mouth."[3]

How is it that these phenomena seem so extreme and bizarre, in fact, so *unfamiliar*? Isn't the act of love a familiar one? Haven't most of us engaged in it many times? The answer to this puzzle involves a sort of dramatic irony. The players on the stage of passion, through the process of sexual arousal, are made unaware of what would be easily apparent to any uninvolved observer. The more aroused you are, the less able you are to perceive what's going on within and around you. Loss of sensory acuity, in fact, is a sure sign of arousal. At the height of passion, love is truly blind. It is also deaf and numb.

Start with the sense of sight. As you meet your lover's

eyes across a candlelit table, your pupils begin to dilate, and your range of vision is narrowed. People passing by might actually disappear from view. At the point of orgasm, you may become practically blind, unable (as experiments have shown) to see bright lights moved directly in front of your open eyes. Hearing is also impaired. At the early stages of excitement, distant sounds begin to fade from awareness. As climax approaches, you may not be able to hear someone shouting only a few feet away. In the same way, your senses of smell, taste, and temperature are numbed. Near orgasm, your whole body may become insensitive to touch and impervious to pain. Lovers engaging in sadomasochistic practices sometimes experience damaging blows as mild tactile stimulation. Lovers involved in "normal" sex are sometimes surprised to find bruises or scratch marks that neither participant can recall having inflicted or received.

During orgasm, in fact, some people fall into complete unconsciousness, which may last a matter of seconds or even minutes—"la petite mort," the little death. Perhaps it is precisely to this condition that all our passion has drawn us, to the place of no-place, the time of no-time. Having arrived at this point of sublime nothingness, we return to the world of ordinary consciousness, realizing only that what we have most desired we can least recall.

CHAPTER TWO

The Primordial Story

THE WORLD is made more of story than of isolated fact. As Borges reminds us, it is only through narrative that our existence takes on its meaning. The labyrinth of nature, he argues, is inherently impenetrable, and the only way we can penetrate it is by creating what he calls "fictions." In any case, it is through story form—in myths, epic poems, and parables, even in history and science, which are rooted in time—that the most profound human knowledge has been transmitted. The close relationship between narrative and knowing can be seen in the history of the words themselves. "Story" goes back to the root of the Greek word *eidenai*, which means "to know." "Narrative" comes from the Greek *gnarare*, which is related to *gnarus*, "knowing, skilled," and thus is also related to "know." Indeed, the human being is not so much the tool-making animal as the story-telling animal.

Every story has its own distinctive rhythm, its periods of rising tension and release. But there seems to be a sort of primordial story form that underlies all traditional stories.

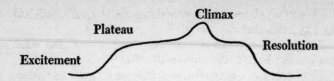

Whatever the subject matter, the style, or the nature of the conflicts and complications involved, the traditional novel, story, play, or tale is likely to create within us a sense of rising excitement followed by lasting fascination, leading at last to a turning point, a climax, which is followed by a resolution. There are, of course, variations; often there are a number of climaxes or subclimaxes. But the basic pattern is just what we see in the process of erotic arousal and consummation. Perhaps, then, the act of love itself is the matrix of the primordial story. In this spirit, I want to cast the extraordinary sequence of events that occurs during lovemaking in story form: as a "fiction." The experiences of Ted and Jan, the young couple in the story that follows, are drawn not from the erotic literature, but from interviews and personal experience. The physiological details come from recent research in sexology, physiology, and endocrinology.[1] The story begins with two exhausted people on the threshold of sleep.

Excitement

Ted and Jan had been married for less than two months. On this warm June night, they were lying, half asleep, on an oversized bed in their small downtown apartment, covered only by a sheet. The windows were open and a gentle breeze ballooned the unlined draperies, through which the glow of city lights dimly lit the room. That their nude bodies were not touching stemmed from no lack of desire to be close. Until this night, in fact, they had slept as if glued together, and their episodes of lovemaking had been both frequent and intense, so much so that they had finally arrived at a state of physical and emotional exhaustion.

"We really have to do something about this," Ted had said at lunch that day.

"I know," Jan laughed. "We keep saying that. But what can we do? I can't keep my hands off of you."

"We've *got* to get some sleep. *I've* got to get some sleep. I'm not getting any work done. I sent out three unsigned letters today. If we don't get some sleep soon—I mean, like tonight—one of us is going to walk out in front of a moving vehicle."

"We should swear a solemn oath we'll go straight to sleep tonight. No lovemaking."

"We've tried solemn oaths," he said.

"Maybe we should sign it in blood," she said.

"Or in semen."

"Oh, no! Here we go again." Her eyes started to laugh, then melted into his.

They were delighted with each other and with the secret knowledge they shared in this public place. That the people at the tables around them couldn't help being aware of their love made the conspiracy even more delicious. At the same time, they were truly ravaged, barely able to keep their eyes open.

That afternoon, as they struggled against sleep at their separate jobs, was even worse, and that night, after having a light dinner before the television set, they were in bed by 8:30. Their plan to go to sleep without even touching each other seemed at last not only possible but necessary and inevitable. Within minutes, they had descended into the dreamy twilight of the theta state, in which their brain waves slowed to around seven cycles a second and their arms and legs seemed to sink of their own weight deep into the mattress.

The vivid, multicolored images that swam in and out of Ted's mind are beyond accurate description, but some vague impulse born of that subterranean carnival caused his arm to extend a few inches so that the back of his relaxed fingers came to rest against the small of Jan's back.

The resilience, temperature, moisture, and barely perceptible movements of that particular part of her body were transmitted toward his brain via a complex system of nerve fibers extending from sensory receptors in the skin of his fingers. At the brain stem (a rich aggregation of gray matter that makes up most of the brain of primitive animals), the incoming messages having to do with his touching her were mixed with additional sensory input. There was information from the semicircular canals of the inner ears concerning his body's orientation in relation to the earth's gravitational field. There was information from the clusters of nerve endings at his body's joints as to the specific angle of each joint, adding up to a subliminal "image" of the configuration of the whole body lying on its right side facing her back. And there were messages from nerve endings in the skin and underlying muscles as to the specific and general pressure between his body and the mattress that supported it. General orienting information of this sort—from the inner ears, joints, skin, and muscles—informs and is essential to all thought and action, and indeed to all coherent brain functioning.

In addition, Ted's brain stem was monitoring any changes in the environment outside his body—and the vital functioning within: heart rate, respiration, blood pressure, blood chemistry, temperature, digestion, peristalsis, and the complex operations of all the internal organs. On this instance, the olfactory nerves at the back of the nasal passages were adding a particularly primitive and poignant sensory input— the mingled odor of her body and his—to the electrochemical messages pulsing into the brain stem and being blended there.

The new information about the feel of Ted's fingers on Jan's back, now coherently patterned in the context of his present condition in space and time, sped from the brain stem to the rest of the brain. There it was compared with memories of his earlier experiences of similar sensations, his cultural conditioning on the matter of touch and erotic arousal, and his experiences with Jan herself. In less than a second, the information had been analyzed and (to use the inadequate language of computer functioning) returned to the brain stem as an operational option.

What happened then might be termed a brief competition between two contrary impulses. On the one hand, the brain's analysis of Ted's blood chemistry argued persuasively for sleep. In fact, a part of the brain stem known as the reticular activating system already was in the process of screening out sensory information about the outside world and helping slow the overall brainwaves from the present seven cycles a second down toward four, which would correspond to the first stages of sleep. On the other hand, the new chain of information that had been triggered by Ted's touching Jan's back argued for a waking experience: exploration, pleasure.

It was a contest of milliseconds and microquantities, decided at levels deeper than thought. A significant turning point occurred at the site of the adrenal glands, which lay like two cocked hats embedded in fat atop the kidneys. Now these glands were getting a direct message, transmitted from the brain through the nervous system, which suggested arousal. So informed, the adrenals put out a powerful mix of hormones that spread with the circulation of the blood throughout Ted's body, starting an increase in heart rate and blood pressure, dilating the blood vessels, stimulating the sweat glands, and thickening the saliva. News of these events, wherever they occurred, was sent back to the brain through intertwining networks of nerve fibers, causing a gradual increase in the tempo of the brain waves. The slowly awakening brain was broadcasting its own commands by way of the nervous system to various parts of the body.

But before Ted was brought to full wakefulness, something happened that holds special significance for our story. As increasing amounts of blood rushed into Ted's penis through its now wide-open arteries, tiny valves in the veins that lead back to the body partially closed. The resulting build-up of blood pressure within the penis caused it to begin to expand. At the same time, the skin of the scrotum thickened and tightened because of congestion of its blood vessels as well as muscular contraction. This tightening helped elevate the testes, which already were being pulled up toward the groin by the shortening of the spermatic cords. The expansion of his penis and contraction of his scrotum created sensations that flashed back through nerve fibers to Ted's brain. The brain analysed these messages, then ordered the adrenals to release even more hormones, thus assuring that the impetus toward arousal would win out over the need for sleep.

Influenced by increased doses of hormones and nerve messages as well, Ted's penis quickly grew to double its previous length, and the head of it pressed against Jan's buttocks. At this, Ted swam into consciousness, and he heard his own unspoken words: "Not *again*." And then, "I must *not* wake Jan up." Still, he made no move to pull back from his wife. His erect penis, throbbing with each beat of his heart, continued pressing against her.

Jan, who also was half-asleep, became aware of this pulsating pressure at a level deeper than consciousness. Over the next thirty seconds or so, her nervous system and endocrine glands performed almost exactly as Ted's had a short time earlier. Her first sexual reaction took place deep within the vagina, where a sweatlike lubricating substance appeared all along the inner walls. Since very few nerve endings exist there, Jan's brain received no significant news of this development.

A few seconds later, however, a sequence of events began that Jan could not ignore, even in her somewhat somnolent state. Involuntary muscular contractions of muscle fibers within her nipples caused them to become erect. Moments later, the breasts themselves began swelling slightly because of the engorgement of blood vessels near the surface. At the same time, the labia majora, the larger, outer lips of the vagina, began opening and thinning out, while the labia minora, the smaller, inner lips, began growing in size, thus adding to the overall length of the vagina. The shaft of Jan's clitoris began expanding in diameter as its blood supply increased, and its head began swelling slightly so that the tiny, sensitive organ fit tightly in its hood, with its tip extending just outside.

Suspended between sleep and arousal, Jan breathed deeply, then sighed audibly. She was vaguely aware that something was happening but had no words or images for it. As if drugged, she felt herself on the verge of a dizzy fall toward unconsciousness, but something pulled her back. She felt a momentary urge to open her eyes; the lids were too heavy. Something was going on in the universe of her body, a gentle, rhythmic contraction of the muscles of her buttocks, pelvis, and thighs, subtle yet powerful beyond her power to control. With that motion, she experienced a warm melting through the center of her.

"What?" she whispered fuzzily, groping for some meaning in unwilled movement and alien sensations. And then, softly, "Oh."

Rising toward full consciousness, Jan realized at last that her husband's penis was pressing against her. The realization brought her attention to a burning focus on that point of contact.

"For a minute I didn't—" she said. "Now I—" She stopped trying to talk, her words seeming not just unnecessary but totally beside the point. She reached behind her and took her husband's penis in her hands.

"We really shouldn't," he said. "We can't."

"I know, darling," she said thickly, aware that her mouth was filling with thick, creamy saliva. "Just let me kiss you. Just for *two* minutes. Then we'll go to sleep." She turned to him, nestled within his arms, and pressed her mouth to his.

Ted's eyes were wide open now. As his wife rolled over, her body glowed in the pale city light. The sound she made

29

as her lips came to his, a childlike cry containing both delight and anguish, penetrated straight to his heart. He felt at that moment he could never get enough of her, even if they lived to be a hundred. He ran his hands over her body, feeling a filmy sheen of perspiration between her breasts and at the small of her neck. Had it been light enough, he would have noticed a pinkish flush breaking out on her skin in both these areas, and on her face as well. And he would have seen as well as felt that all the rounded surfaces of her body had become even rounder and fuller. But now everything seemed all new, as if he had never touched her before. The movements of his hands seemed slow and dreamlike; time and space were beginning to expand.

As Jan kissed her husband more and more deeply, the metamorphosis of her body continued. The inner two-thirds of her vagina began lengthening and dilating in irregular, tension-less pulses. Her cervix began pulling upward, thus opening her vagina even wider at its deepest end. At the same time, the secretion of vaginal lubricating fluid became so copious that it began oozing out and wetting the entire area around the entryway to her vagina.

Hardly aware of what she was doing, Jan reached down and brought Ted's penis betwen her legs. The involuntary motion of their bodies fell into a rhythm. He kissed her cheeks, her eyes, her nose, then took her mouth again. The head of his penis slid back and forth across her clitoris, her inner lips, and the mouth of her vagina. They breathed together in quickening gasps and sighs. Their hearts beat with equal and synchronous intensity. Sleep, which only a few minutes earlier had seemed such an urgent need, now was entirely out of the question.

Plateau

For Jan and Ted, the transition between the stages in our story that have been designated "excitement" and "plateau" was marked only by a mutual and full acceptance that their love would now have its way despite their earlier resolve to the contrary.

"I'm sorry," Ted said thickly.

"I'm glad," Jan said.

"I love you," they both said in a single voice.

During the months of their joining, such moments of synchrony had become almost commonplace, but they took each one as further validation of their connectedness. Ted felt an electric thrill rise in his groin and course upward through his trunk, downward to his toes. Every last reservation fell away, and nothing was left but a pure and simple desire to *know* his wife, to become totally one with her. All doubts were gone. The sense of potence and certitude that had started with the aching fullness of his penis now surged through his entire body.

Just then, the two small Cowper's glands that nestled against the urethra just below Ted's prostrate shot a few drops of clear, slippery liquid into the urethra. A moment later, two drops of the liquid appeared at the tip of Ted's penis, where it mingled with the lubricating fluid that continued oozing from Jan's vagina. This preorgasmic fluid had no effect on Ted's erection, which remained firm and constant. His right testicle already was drawn up against his body, and the lower, left testicle rose upward too.

The plateau-stage changes in Jan's body were far more complex. The areolae of her breasts swelled so as to partially hide her erect nipples. The entire breasts continued growing fuller and more rounded, while a rosy mottling spread over them, starting at the bottom and fanning up and outward. The inner lips of her vagina continued swelling. Now more than two times their normal diameter, they were beginning to protrude beyond the outer lips and were nearly ready for the vivid color shift that was to come. Meanwhile, Jan's clitoris was beginning to retract within its hood; already the tip had disappeared. During intercourse, the clitoris would be stimulated not by direct contact with the penis, but by friction of the encapsulating tissues connected to the vagina's

31

inner lips. The inner two-thirds of Jan's vagina was continuing to open wider. But it was different in the outer third, where the lining was becoming engorged with blood, thus creating a soft, labile orgasmic platform, which had the effect of reducing the diameter of the opening.

Jan's breaths were coming faster, and her muscles were contracting and relaxing in an uncontrollable rhythm. She felt an even deeper sensation of certainty and power than her husband felt. She was vaguely aware of the fullness and the increased sensitivity of her breasts and groin, the spontaneous sliding of her hand over her husband's body. The words "consumed by passion" passed through her mind.

"Won't you please come into me?" she begged. "We won't take much time—not tonight. Please."

"Of course, of course," Ted whispered.

She rolled over on top of him and drew her knees up around his hips. She reached down and put the head of his penis into her. She remained poised there for a moment, overwhelmed by the intensity of feeling in the outer third of her vagina. The fullness of his organ and hers made for a snugness, a resistance to further entry, that inflamed them both. With an urge deeper than thought, Ted wanted to penetrate his wife to the core, to destroy whatever might prevent the two of them from merging completely. Jan shared in this desire for the devastation of anything that might keep them apart. After what seemed an extended interlude measured only partially by time, Jan moved impulsively to take Ted's penis into her all the way to the hilt, unaware of the visceral cry that was a precise description in sound of that motion and the sensation it produced.

The two lovers fell into a familiar rhythmic undulation that provided the maximum stimulation for both. A few minutes earlier, the two tiny Bartholin's glands within Jan's inner lips had secreted one drop each of liquid at the entrance to her vagina. This had helped to ease the entry of Ted's penis, but its vigorous motion was lubricated mostly by the copious secretion that continued flowing from the walls of

Jan's vagina. Without altering the rhythm, Jan lifted her pelvis so that she could look down and watch Ted's penis going in and out of her. Even in the dimness, its liquid gleam was faintly visible.

At the same time, unseen and unknown by either lover, a remarkable transmutation was taking place at the site of Jan's most intense pleasure. The inner lips and clitoral hood, normally (as with most women who have not yet had children) a salmon pink hue, was shifting rapidly to a brilliant red. This florid coloration was a sure sign that Jan was on her way to orgasm. As the lovers' movements became faster and more urgent, in fact, every other sign of her readiness was fully realized. Her clitoris, now only half its normal length, was retracted deep within its hood. The orgasmic platform lining the outer third of her vagina was fully engorged, while the deeper cavity was open wide and the cervix was drawn up as high as it could go. Every muscle in her body was pulsing. Her face was flushed, her blood was racing, and her heart was beating nearly three times every second.

As Jan raised her upper body and flung back her head to gasp for breath, Ted saw her breasts, now a fourth larger than their normal size, splendidly displayed in the shadowless light. His body was also fully prepared for orgasm. Both testes, grown half again larger than usual, were drawn up tight between his legs. His penis, already full length when he had entered her, had become somewhat thicker, especially at the coronal ridge that circles its head. The thrusts of his pelvis and the movements of his hands over his wife's body has passed beyond his control. He was only vaguely aware of the sounds that he and she were making. All of him was swept up in a maelstrom that the two of them had somehow created out of their exhaustion and desire. As if from a great distance, he heard her crying out that she could wait no longer. At that moment, he felt something melting, giving way, at the very center of his being.

Insofar as he was aware of specific physical events, Ted knew that now nothing could prevent his ejaculation. This sense of inevitability came from a complex series of events already in progress within his body. As his powerful, thrusting movements continued, seminal fluid containing millions of sperm cells was being propelled out of his testes through the rhythmic contractions of a convoluted mass of some fifteen small vessels at the top of each. The fluid traveled slowly up two narrow but thick-walled tubes called the vas deferens, which run in the spermatic cords through the inguinal canals on either side of the groin and then descend into the pelvis to be joined by two more fluid-producing glands called the seminal vesicles. Millions of sperm cells already were gathered at this juncture. Both the vas deferens and the seminal vesicles were pulsing with strong contractions deep inside Ted's body, shooting two kinds of seminal fluid into the prostatic urethra. And the prostate itself was contracting rhythmically, adding its own milky fluid to the seminal mix. By this time, the internal sphincter of the bladder had closed tight to keep any urine from getting into the seminal fluid and also to prevent a backward seminal ejaculation into the bladder. And a few inches farther along, the urethral bulb at the root of the penis had swelled to nearly three times its normal size in anticipation of the flood of fluid that was soon to come.

It was all this internal activity that made Ted feel that nothing on heaven or earth could stop him from ejaculating. Within three seconds from the onset of this feeling, the external sphincter of Ted's bladder relaxed and semen poured into the swollen urethral bulb and then coursed on through the penile urethra, propelled by contractions along the floor of the pelvis and within the penis itself. In forceful pulsations separated by less than a second, semen shot from Ted's penis into his wife's vagina as he held her close to him. The first few pulsations were entirely out of Ted's control. After that, the contractions that had wracked his body became less intense, and Ted prolonged his pleasure by consciously tightening his pelvis muscles in rhythm with the waning pulsations.

Jan's orgasm was not so complex as her husband's, but no less profound. It began with a single involuntary spasm of the engorged outer third of her vagina, at which point she knew that a full orgasm was inevitable. As she cried out that she could wait no longer, a warm, melting sensation spread from her pelvis, suffusing through her entire body, and within seconds she was overwhelmed by powerful vaginal and pelvic contractions, closely synchronized with Ted's. As her body pulsed and rippled deep inside, her cries joined those of her husband. It was a sound for which our language has no adequate words.

Resolution

Before her orgasm was entirely finished, the areolae around Jan's nipples began losing their swelling and quickly took on a corrugated appearance, with the nipples remaining sharply erect. As her contractions subsided, Jan simply went limp and lay sobbing softly on her husband's chest. Their bodies seemed glued together by the various liquids that covered them from head to toe, and their hearts drummed together, now seeking a slower beat. Within seconds, the metamorphosis of Jan's body began reversing itself. Once again, the tip of her clitoris emerged from beneath its hood. Her inner vaginal lips quickly shrank to normal size and began fading in color, from brilliant red to their usual pink. In seconds more, the swollen lining of the outer third of her vagina took on its normal configuration, thus increasing the diameter of the vaginal opening. At the same time, Ted's penis went from fully erect to only half erect.

As the lovers' breathing began slowing, their consciousness, too, began returning to normal. It was as if they had been to some distant place, exotic yet familiar. Regaining awareness of her surroundings, Jan realized that tears were streaming from her eyes and falling on her husband's face. She heard his voice as if from far away, unbearably intimate.

"Oh, God, it was—"

"I know. I know," she murmured.

Still moved by forces beyond their conscious control, the two lovers found their mouths joined in a lingering kiss. Before the kiss ended, Jan realized that her husband had fallen into a deep sleep. Carefully and quietly, she slipped off him and lay nestled close, one leg drawn up over him, her face still wet with tears. Within seconds, she too was asleep.

As Ted and Jan lay sleeping, the reverse metamorphosis of their bodies continued. Ted's scrotum gradually relaxed and the spermatic cord lengthened, while his testes shrank to normal size. His penile urethra shortened at the same rate that his penis became smaller, and the expanded bulb at the root of it narrowed to its normal diameter. His heart rate and respiration dropped to those levels common to deep sleep. Jan's physiological process paralleled that of her husband. Her nipples gradually lost their erection, became soft and pliant. The additional breast volume that had accompanied arousal began melting away, as did the added roundness of cheeks, lips, shoulders, arms, belly, hips, and legs. The pink flush of her skin faded. The diameter of her clitoris was gradually reduced. The inner two-thirds of her vagina that had opened wide during the act of love began closing. In this process, the cervix, the neck of the womb, descended so that the mouth of it dipped into the pool of semen that had collected in the depths of Jan's vagina. This event, which was to be an especially significant one, took place several minutes after wife and husband had lost all conscious awareness.

CHAPTER THREE

An Explosion of the Spirit

IF THIS STORY of love has a physical dimension, it has a spiritual one as well, no less profound. Let us now go back to the moment during plateau when Jan moved impulsively to take Ted's penis all the way into her vagina, letting out a visceral cry as she did so.

Ted was not entirely unaware of that sound, but it came to him as a soft detonation, a sort of slow-motion explosion in his consciousness. After that, it was as if he had entered an area of calm within a maelstrom, the eye of the hurricane. The slide of his penis within Jan seemed to slow, so he could savor every millimeter of that motion. At the same time, the distinction between his genitals and the rest of his body began to blur. He was only vaguely aware of his exertions. More and more, he experienced himself as having entered, through Jan's body, something open and spacious, where no discriminations were possible—not between body and spirit, or pleasure and pain.

At the same time, Jan was extraordinarily sensitive to the movements of her husband's penis inside her. It was as if he were first filling her entire pelvic area, then her belly and breasts and thighs, then all of her, every cell. This feeling of being totally filled was so strange that Jan lifted her pelvis so that she could look down and watch Ted's penis going in and out of her and see if it was still only in one place rather than everywhere inside her. Without having altered her rhythm, she pressed her pelvis down on her husband's body again and closed her eyes. The image remained—a gleaming, thrusting penis vivid in her consciousness—and she simply let go all her resistance to the incredible. Yes, there was a single penis filling only one part of her, and also filling all of her, every cell. With this surrender, Jan sensed herself opening even wider deep inside, relinquishing her body itself. Now there was nothing left of her, no boundaries at all. Without realizing what she was doing, she raised her upper body and flung back her head to gasp for breath.

Ted's eyes were wide open, but he only dimly perceived the image of his wife's breasts and throat. He was only vaguely aware of the sounds that he and she were making. His consciousness was almost entirely occupied with the experience of having entered an enormous space, perhaps as large as the universe itself. There was also the possibility that there existed some experience beyond his body and hers, beyond this universe. He knew he was making love to his wife, and he was also somewhere else, being drawn toward an ultimate, shining darkness. He was afraid of going farther into this darkness, yet he was unwilling to turn back. As if from a great distance, he heard Jan crying out that she could wait no longer. At this moment, he felt something melting, giving away, at the very center of his being. He knew that now nothing in heaven or earth could stop him, and he was swept into the delicious dark, aware only of pulsations that seemed to go on forever. Finally, he felt himself coming back to his body, to the experience of something flowing from him into his wife. To slow time, he contracted the muscles of his pelvis in rhythm with the pulsations that had carried him away. He brought back to this world only echoes of the void, fading memories of the dark.

For Jan, there had been no space and time at all, only an almost unbearable sense of love and oneness. With her deepest knowing, she knew that even the tiniest atom within her was filled with her husband. Nothing separate was left of her, yet strangely she was more herself, more powerful and certain, than ever. With her first contractions, she began crying aloud, the tears that flowed from her eyes matching the flow of liquid into her body. It was as if she always had been crying and would cry forever. As the powerful contractions of her body subsided, she went limp and lay sobbing softly on her husband's chest. She heard his voice and her own as if from far away, not the words but the music of it.

"Oh, God, it was—"

"I know. I know."

Still moved by forces beyond their conscious control, the two lovers found their mouths joined in a lingering kiss. Before the kiss had ended, Jan realized that her husband had fallen into a deep sleep. She slipped off him and lay nestled close, her face still wet with tears. Within seconds, she too was asleep.

An Incredible Atomic Dance

A little less than five minutes after Jan's orgasm, as she and her husband lay sleeping, the neck of her womb descended from its elevated position and dipped into the pool of semen that had collected deep inside her vagina. Millions of spermatozoa at once began their perilous journey up the cervical canal and into the womb. It was a mad carnival of confusion, disablement, and death. Each of the tiny cells with their streamlined bodies and long, wildly thrashing tails had a message of creation to deliver against impossible odds. Casualties were everywhere, victims of topography, bacteria, and the acid content of the sea in which they swam. Survivors

39

struggled over the dead bodies of their fellows only to suc-cumb themselves or become so exhausted they simply drifted with the current. Yet the cloud of sperm cells continued their journey.

Three hours passed for the sleeping lovers, a third of an effective lifetime for the microscopic swimmers. A vanguard had somehow made its way up to the very top of the womb and into the funnellike opening of one of the Fallopian tubes. There it came upon a large, round cell, the unknown goal of all the voyaging. Thousands of sperm cells pressed against the egg, seeking entry. Finally, through a process of selection not yet understood, one of them was allowed to pass through two membranes and into a magical interior sea.

In contrast to the insane confusion and random savagery of the long journey, all was elegant, stately, and measured inside. Once penetrated, the membranes of the egg changed their composition so as not to admit any other sperm; even the tail of the entering sperm cell was left outside. Thus, absolute privacy was assured for the ceremony that was to follow. It was as formal as a minuet and infinitely more in-tricate. Slowly, the sperm and the female pronucleus floated toward one another. The sperm rotated as it moved so that its centrosome would be positioned precisely between itself and its oncoming mate. During this part of the dance, the sperm went through an astonishing metamorphosis, becom-ing ten times larger and spherical, a perfect match for the female pronucleus. The centrosome divided and separated, drawing a veil of fine connective strands between the two converging nuclei, which helped them come closer.

And now the two nuclei moved together to become one. What the lovers who produced them had achieved in their consciousness, the nuclei would achieve in the magical realm of molecules, atoms, and elementary particles. Merging, the nuclei lost their separate boundaries. The male and female chromosomes inside them—long, helical molecules contain-ing enough information to make a human being, yet each incomplete without its counterpart—met and joined and twined around one another, trading information that went back to the beginning of time and up to the moment of conception of the two sleeping lovers, creating out of this interchange something new in the universe: in silence and darkness, a shining affirmation.

PART II

Love's Promise

CHAPTER FOUR

How I Learned About Sex

MY FATHER was a powerful man. Through word and deed, he taught me to trust him completely. He taught me that he knew everything or, at the least, that he knew all that was worth knowing. Without words, he let me know that fears, doubts, and weaknesses were not to be revealed. This unspoken injunction had the force of a primitive taboo; early in life I came to believe that a weakness, once expressed, becomes real.

But this is not the familiar parental horror story, the Freudian rationalization for a misspent life. To the contrary, I remember my father with joy and appreciation. He gave me genuine love, support, and respect. He offered me the dignity of my own absolute individuality. He told me many times that while "they" might take away all that I could accumulate in money and material goods (I grew up in the Depression years), "they" could never take away "what you have inside," by which he meant the possessions of the spirit: knowledge, imagination, music.

Regarding his relationship to me, my father was direct and clear: "I want you to know, son, that whatever happens, whatever you do or become, I'll always be *with you*, one hundred percent." He meant these words to the depth of his soul and the limits of his ability. In later years, even during periods when my views were anathema to him, his support for me, whether moral or substantive, remained strong and certain.

During my childhood, I basked in my father's love and admiration. He took me on his business trips in the summer: endless rides down sunbaked Georgia highways to make calls on his local agents. (He was an insurance *executive*, he told me, not just an *agent*.) Any doubts or fears he might have had were invisible to me. I saw only strength: his powerful hands lying gently on the steering wheel as he guided the car at speeds far above the limit. I sat next to him in perfect peace. Though my eyes were on the road, I was aware of his glowing brown eyes, his aquiline nose, his neat brown mustache, the debonair smile that played around the edges of his lips as he thought of something amusing or impressive to tell me. I was sometimes embarrassed by the extravagance of his talk, but his agents obviously loved it. "Your daddy's a man," one of them told me, "that when he walks in a room, everybody sits up and takes notice." His confidence and strength, validated wherever he went, made a fortress for me in a world that often seemed scary and threatening.

Therefore, the first time I ever saw my father uncertain and even shaken was a momentous event in my life. It was after supper on a spring evening of my eleventh year. He asked me to come out to the front porch. He sat. I sat. He started to say something, then paused. He looked worried. My heart began beating faster.

"Son," he said at last, "there's something I want to talk to you about."

"All right," I said, feeling an inexplicable chill at the pit of my stomach.

Again there was a pause. Something new and frightening

was entering my world. Whatever he had to talk about, if it could have this effect on *him*, must be truly terrible.

"I just want to tell you about . . . self-abuse. Do you know what that is?"

"Yes," I said under my breath. I had no idea what he was talking about but never considered asking him; you don't reveal your ignorance. In any case, I wanted the scene over with. To see my confident, all-knowing father in this state was shivering the foundations of my existence. Worse yet was the realization that there might be something in the world bigger and stronger than he, something even he couldn't handle.

He spoke again, not looking at me. The normally powerful, forthright eyes were angled down toward the floor. "You should never abuse yourself—" His eyes met mine briefly. We both looked away. "You should never abuse yourself because . . . it might someday keep you from becoming a father. . . . Do you understand?"

"Yes," I whispered, not understanding at all, but willing to do or say anything to get it over with.

"All right," he said, relieved that he had done his duty and would have to go no further. "I just wanted to be sure you knew."

How brief it was, my introduction to sex, how lacking in drama. Nothing here to match some of the stories related by the people I've interviewed for this book. One attractive, sexually active woman in her early thirties, for example, told me that when she was putting on her makeup for her first date, her father burst into the bathroom, took out his penis and started waving it at her. "Do you see this? That's all they want to do—just stick this in you. That's all they want. Do you get that?" Nor could my father's little talk compare with certain literary scenes—say the hellfire sermon in James Joyce's *A Portrait of the Artist as a Young Man*, in which a priest at a religious retreat describes the torments that await those who surrender to carnal desire.

47

Every sense of the flesh is tortured and every faculty of the soul therewith: the eyes with impenetrable utter darkness, the nose with noisome odours, the ears with yells and howls and execrations, the taste with foul matter, leprous corruption, nameless suffocating filth, the touch with redhot goads and spikes, with cruel tongues of flame. And through the several torments of the senses, the immortal soul is tortured eternally in its very essence. . . .

Next to these examples, my father's words were mild indeed. Yet the woman whose father waved his penis at her was having sexual relations within months of the episode. And Joyce's young hero, Stephen Dedalus, though convinced and thoroughly frightened by the priest's words, falls again into the joys of the flesh within a few pages.

My reaction was quite different, and for good reasons. The girl's father was someone she could hate and thus reject. My father, on the other hand, was someone I loved and admired, someone who could do no wrong. How could I reject him or ignore what he told me for my own good? Joyce's priest was in total command of his subject; he stood somehow above it, sustained by the mighty authority of the Church. The force of the erotic was great, but by no means greater than he. My introduction to the subject, on the other hand, led me to believe that this force—*whatever it was*—was larger, more mysterious, and more powerful than even my previously omniscient, omnipotent father. How could I toy with a force of such magnitude?

Though I didn't know what "self-abuse" meant when my father first used the term, I had a vague feeling it had to do with the part of my body that no one ever touched or mentioned. Then, too, each of us is possessed of a knowledge deeper than thought. Even while my father was speaking, this veiled knowledge had manifested itself in a sinking sensation that moved down through my abdomen to my groin.

The upshot was that all through my childhood and adolescence I never masturbated. This involved, I must say, no dramatic, agonizing struggle against temptation. It wasn't even a question of being tempted or *not* being tempted, but something beyond that. The repression, for me, was so deep that the possibility never rose to consciousness. Nor could my abstinence be attributed to a lack of desire. Just to glimpse the unexpected silhouette of a girl's breast across the aisle at school was enough to produce an immediate and lasting arousal. It seems I spent most of my time at school in a state of tumescence, in constant dread that I might be called on by the teacher to stand up. But nothing specific was needed to cause an erection. It was simply that a part of my body was often out of my control, liable to change shape and size at the unlikeliest and most inconvenient times.

Spring and summer were especially cruel. On those shimmering, sultry Georgia days, seeing a pretty girl was like being hit between the eyes. Her face and body would shine as if from within. The surrounding world would also become luminous, so bright that my vision would begin to break up and my head would spin. And there was nothing I could do about it. All hope seemed to lie in some distant, incredible future. Along with my father's injunction against masturbation there was a romantic promise about the joys of married love. One happy, carefree day when my father and I were driving down a curving dirt road toward a river bottom crowded with ripe corn, he said, "What you'll do with your wife will be the most beautiful thing any man can experience."

What was he talking about. *What* could I do? I had no way of finding out. Remember, you didn't admit not knowing something. I was too proud to ask my friends about the mechanics of sex, and when they asked if I knew, I always said yes. It was not until I was nearly fourteen that I puzzled out how the act was performed, and even then I could conjure up no clear picture of it.

So instead of specific knowledge and experience, I had a

whole world that was erotic: the hum of insects, the song of birds, my sister's laughter, the feel of sun on skin, the sinuous, slow-motion swing of oak boughs in the wind. Sometimes on those summer days, I looked at the way a tall, straight pine tree was thrust into the earth, the power and intimacy of that joining, and once more I would become dizzy with wonder and frustration and desire. I knew only that there was a force, a powerful erotic force, that permeated all things. With every cell of my body, I longed for—*what*? I was in love with, in lust with, the whole world.

What could I do? My body handled the situation. Almost every night, it seemed, I had a wet dream. Even so, the repression continued to work very well: I never remembered the dreams. And no one ever mentioned the subject. Our culture had taught us well, prescribing silence and denial for almost everything that deeply touched our lives.

But my father was above all a man of action. When I was fourteen, without telling me exactly why, he took me to the family doctor, a fat, light-skinned man who might have served as the model for a Norman Rockwell country doctor.

"Do you touch yourself at night?" he asked, as my father stood worriedly by.

"No," I answered, shaking my head fervently.

"Are any dreams associated with it?"

"No." Again I shook my head.

The doctor glanced at my father. Obviously they had discussed the matter.

"Well, I don't think it's serious," the doctor said. "Maybe you should try drinking less water or milk near bedtime."

That was it. We left with no further discussion. But there had been one small ray of hope. When the doctor had asked me about dreams, his eyes had twinkled slightly. In that twinkle lay my salvation. Maybe it wasn't the worst thing in the world after all.

Many years later, I learned that one of my younger brothers had had a somewhat similar experience. At about age eleven, he had developed the habit of taking an hour or more to get dressed in the morning. One morning my father came into his room with a worried look on his face and asked if during these periods he abused himself. Like me, my brother had no idea what the term meant. Thinking it referred to his dawdling, his waste of time, he answered, "I guess I do." My father's shoulders slumped in defeat. He shook his head sadly and walked out of the room.

In any case, both my brother and I survived the repression with no permanent ill effects. Gradually my unremembered dreams became less frequent, and I married young, a virgin, just as my father and his Victorian doctrine would have it. Since starting my researches for this book, I've looked into many of the writings of present-day sex reformers and interviewed a number of experts on the subject. They would probably be unanimous in condemning the kind of repression I suffered. And I find it hard to disagree. In a more enlightened milieu, I might well have enjoyed a relaxed and fulfilling sex life as a teenager. The power of my libido would have been released, and I would have entered marriage with more experience and perspective. More practiced, more casual about sex, I probably wouldn't have put such high demands on married love, a heavy burden to be sure. And I would probably have tempered my romanticism with that benign cynicism that informs and lubricates all long-term relationships.

But I wonder. What if I had become sexually liberated as a teenager? In my crowd, sex probably would have been hurried and difficult, exploitative, trivial. Then, too, there is something to be said for as well as against sublimation. I bring to mind those successful teenage studs of my acquaintance, the early maturers who had it made, who settled back smugly into the easy competence of their bodies. Not for them the restless energy that drove me into mad passions for one hobby after another—nature study, chemistry, amateur radio, flying, music—the interests that have shaped my life and career.

What I'm trying to say here is that any ideological position, be it Victorian or counter-Victorian, must eventually fail, especially in the realm of the erotic. The problem with ideology is that it attempts to set life in concrete while the erotic remains forever fluid, destroying categories, and defying simple solutions. I think of my father and his brief introduction to sex and I fail to muster up an iota of resentment. The love and freedom that he and my mother and aunt and sister gave me far outweigh any misguided words he might have spoken. In any case, factual knowledge can contribute to enlightenment but is not to be confused with it. My erotic journey was just beginning. And there was another thing: a situation in my family that was to confront me with what is perhaps the ultimate paradox in the erotic realm.

CHAPTER FIVE

Familiar Love

WHEN I WAS THREE, the maiden aunt who was to live with my family during most of my childhood took me out to the back yard and suggested I plant an acorn. If I did, she told me, it would grow to be as big as the tree beneath which we stood. I looked up. The huge trunk, the vertiginous branches, seemed to reach to the clouds.

"Will it really?" I asked.

"Yes, it will," she said, laughing. "Just that big."

I remember the feel of that acorn in my hand, alive with potency. The world was large and wonderful. I dug a little hole and planted the acorn. My aunt showed me how to water it. Every day I watched for the tree to begin growing.

At about the same time, my father and mother told me I was going to have a little sister. There was no explanation of where she would come from or what she would be like— another mystery. A couple came to visit my parents. They had just attended a children's dance recital and had the program with them. On the cover was a picture of an adorable little girl about my age, a tap dancer, wearing black sequinned tights.

"Pretty soon," somebody told me, "you're going to have a little sister just like her."

My reaction must have been amusing, for I remember everyone laughing as I stared, transfixed, at the picture. I took the program and kept it in my room. Again and again I looked at the picture: the sequinned tap dancer, the little sister who would soon come to live with me. If there is romantic love at three, I was in love with that sister.

When my mother went to the hospital (what a strange place to get a sister!), I was left with my aunt. There was a dreamy interlude, enveloped in silence, indefinite in hours and minutes. After I was in bed, my father came home with the news that I had a little sister. In a day or two I would go to the hospital to see her.

I can remember that particular room in Emory University Hospital in Atlanta, Georgia, almost as clearly as the living room of my own house: the single bed against the far wall, the window at the right of the bed with late morning sunlight streaming in, the scales just inside the door, flowers in vases all around. And there was my mother in the bed, a pretty woman wearing a pink negligee, fully made up. Nestled in her left arm was something bundled in blankets. My father lifted me up for a better view, and my mother pushed back the blankets so that I could see my sister.

I was horrified. Expecting sequins and a romantic pose, I was confronted with the most repulsive living thing I had ever seen. The head seemed lopsided, the features compressed and confused. There was a yellowish cast to the skin.

Did I weep? Did I voice my horror? All I can remember is confusion, aching disappointment, a sense of having been fooled. I wanted to go home as soon as I could.

Childhood Love

Sister (we all came to call her that) was an easy baby. We had a black maid as well as my aunt to help care for the

54

children, so my mother could linger in the Victorian role of semi-invalid, a vaguely feminine creature beset by vague nervous disorders. Every morning, my father strode forth like a knight into battle, returning in the evening to his close little family, jaunty and victorious. The wizened, yellowish infant I had seen at the hospital went through a spectacular metamorphosis. With her large, bright eyes, full cheeks and ready smile, she was soon stopping passersby on the street. Very early her eyes began darkening; she would take after my father. Throughout her life, I found it hard to understand how such deep, dark eyes could glow from within, as if powered by some internal source.

Maggie, our maid, let me carry my baby sister. I would walk her around the house or the yard, then sit and let her grasp my finger in her hand. I felt unbearable tenderness. I forgot about my sequinned tap dancer. I was never jealous; she was too much "mine," a part of me.

Sister rarely cried. But sometimes, when she hurt herself and began screaming with a baby's utter lack of self-consciousness and reserve, a strange thing would happen to me. It was as if something invaded me, took over my diaphragm and lungs and vocal cords. I, a four-year-old, would scream along with my baby sister. Tears would pour from my eyes. I would nearly faint from lack of breath. And yet, the "I" inside me was not involved in this violent act at all, but rather witnessing it, trying, in fact, to stop it. Several months were to pass before I learned to control my own breathing while my sister was crying.

Even then, the two of us were connected in a way that was somehow both visceral and mystical. We created a special, smaller circle in the circle of the family. Though nearly four years separated us, we grew together, almost as twins. At the dinner table, no cross words were spoken by the grown-ups, but a powerful force-field emanated from the unspoken hostility between my mother and my aunt (who was my father's sister) and from the unresolved frustration between my mother and father. The rays from this field of silence might have destroyed the tissue of our lives. But we sat across from each other and created a magic bubble of intimacy. Nothing could penetrate it. We were invulnerable.

What we did, in fact, was to make things funny. I could get Sister to laugh at almost anything I said. Our game was for me to make her burst into uncontrollable laughter just as she took a drink of milk so that the milk would spray all over the table. If my timing was really good (disgusting children!), she would laugh so explosively that milk would shoot out of her nostrils. But the grown-ups weren't really disgusted. Our effervescent laughter, our innocent naughtiness, relieved their tensions. They scolded us but laughed as they did so.

My sister remembers her childhood as "totally happy." In spite of the undercurrents, there was a sense of fun in our family. We were "special"—the descendants on my father's side of English nobility, of Colonial governors, of the illustrious and deliciously controversial Burrs. My sister and I might have looked around at our physical surroundings in vain for signs of our aristocratic heritage, but we didn't look and we didn't question. Material things weren't important anyway. Wherever *we* lived was perfect. Whatever *we* did was right.

Not for us the summer camps our friends attended. We always had our *own* country place. We had, as a matter of fact, a whole series of country places: a log cabin on five wooded acres, a shack on the banks of the Chattahoochee River, a concrete-block house by a small lake, a larger brown frame house on a hundred acres of woods and tenant-farmed corn and cotton fields. As soon as one of these places was brought to a satisfactory state of completion, our father, manifesting his restless nature, would sell it at a loss and move on to another. In each of these domains, I was prince and my sister was princess.

We went to the country almost every weekend. Sometimes

we took a friend or two along, but mostly it was just mother, father, sister, and brother. (Our long-suffering aunt was not included in these jaunts.) Leaving the city behind, Sister and I, each in our own customary place in the backseat of the family car, would poke fun at other drivers and urge our father to go faster. It would have been unthinkable for anyone to pass us. Sister was uninhibited. If it was a hot summer day when we arrived at the country place, she would take off everything but her underpants and run around "like a little savage," as my mother's mother said sourly. Driving home in the Sunday night darkness, the two of us would sit in silence, secure in each other's presence. There was something strange in our family. (What was that peculiar stiffness in our mother's body as she embraced our father? Why did she cry so much? What was she crying about?) And the outside world seemed somehow threatening. But our father was strong and Sister and I were there together in the back seat, totally aware of each other without conscious awareness. Everything was all right.

Like my father, Sister was dauntless and joyful. Once, when I was about nine, a tennis ball that I and my friends were throwing around fell into an uncovered sewer. We could see the ball lying on the bottom, far beyond our reach. My five-year-old sister came to our rescue. She let two of us hold her by the ankles and lower her, upside down, to the bottom of the sewer so that she could retrieve the ball. After that, whenever a ball went down in the sewer, we summoned Sister to her ordeal.

By the time I was twelve, I was an intrepid naturalist, a hunter and curator, with my friend John Crenshaw, of a large and almost unmanageable collection of snakes and other reptiles. With around a hundred live specimens representing some forty species, we put on periodic neighborhood reptile shows (admission: five cents). We trained Sister to perform, showing her how to let two small snakes coil around her wrists and a larger one coil around her neck. Stripped to her underpants and adorned with three brightly colored serpents, she was worth the price of admission. John and I assumed she enjoyed the experience and loved snakes as we did. It was perhaps forty years later that I learned touching snakes had always made her skin crawl and that she had done it only because she would have done anything I asked her to do.

I was late in learning everything. Sister was early. The day I learned to ride a bicycle, she did too. The day I learned to roller-skate, she got up on her skates, fell innumerable times, and finally, with blood oozing from both knees, skated triumphantly along behind me. We both learned to swim the same day; I was twelve, she was eight. Sister was a tomboy, a tagalong. I have a vivid memory of skating on the sidewalk from one end of my block to the other with my friend, Bobby Hicks, and looking back to see Sister trying to keep up with us, always dropping behind but valiant and determined, leaning forward, skating for all she was worth.

Our parents were blessedly permissive. Perhaps it was mainly because they were so preoccupied with the faltering machinery of their own relationship. (By the time I was six, my mother was well into what was called a "nervous breakdown" that was to last many years.) In any case, they forced nothing on us and approved of almost everything we did. This permissiveness was the despair of my mother's mother, a stern, religious woman, a strict disciplinarian. When we visited our maternal grandparents in their big white house in the little town of Monroe, Georgia, our grandmother (we called her Murr) would take our mother to task. It was an absolute disgrace, she said, how my mother let us run wild, do anything we wanted, say anything we wanted. What we needed, Murr told my mother, was "a dose of Doctor Green." By this, she meant that we needed to be smartly whipped with a long, green switch.

It was when I was about nine or ten, I think, that Murr's continual prodding became more than my mother could bear. I committed some verbal sin, perhaps failing to say m'am to Murr, and my mother came at me with a switch, leaned over, and started rather ineffectually whipping my lower legs. I stood there, put my hands on my hips and looked down at her scornfully. She kept at it for a few seconds, then burst into tears and ran back to her room. Not long after that, I heard screams from the back of the house. I ran as fast as I could to the source of the sound, burst into the large latticed back porch, and saw to my horror that Murr herself was giving Sister a dose of Doctor Green, ripping away at her bare legs with a long, mean-looking, green switch. Sister's face was contorted with pain. She was screaming and trying to avoid the blows.

What happened brought back those earlier times when Sister's crying had triggered my own. It was as if some force invaded me and took control of my body. I witnessed myself running over and leaping on Murr's back. As Murr was later to describe it ad nauseam and totally without humor, "That little imp of Satan rode me to the ground. He rode me to the ground." The action was decisive. Neither Murr nor anyone else ever tried to spank Sister again.

We never talked about how much we loved each other. It was beyond that.

A Troubling Metamorphosis

When I was fourteen and Sister was ten, something strange started happening. I found myself getting annoyed at her mannerisms. Sometimes she seemed smug and grandiose; at other times she was merely sullen. She made her cheeks hollow, her mouth long and thin, producing an expression that I called her "wolf look." To Sister's dismay, the whole family took up the term. Then there was something else. At our country place one summer day, our father called Sister in and made her put on a blouse. One of my friends had accompanied us, and Sister was obviously developing breasts.

She complained bitterly about her loss of freedom, but Daddy was stern. It was her first real encounter with injustice. She became even more sullen. Her wolf look deepened. We began quarreling. My annoyance seemed to me, even then, curiously disproportionate.

But this unhappy interlude was to be short-lived. Even the darkest hormones of puberty were no match for Sister's ebullience and lovingness. She emerged from sullenness into something far more disturbing. My little sister, my visceral and psychic twin, the person closer to me than anyone else in the universe, was becoming an erotically desirable female. She blossomed with startling speed. Her breasts continued to grow. Her waist seemed to become even smaller; her skin became smoother. Her eyes became even larger, even darker, even shinier. Most people thought she was the prettiest girl in her class. She was certainly the most desirable.

All this happened at the most difficult possible time for me. At fifteen and sixteen, I was a confused mass of unfocused lust, unsure even of the boundaries of my body and being. The whole world was erotic, but I had no way of touching it. It was not that I reached out and ended up empty-handed—I didn't even know how to reach out. It was not that I asked and was refused—I didn't even know how to ask. I had no hands and arms. I was mute. Even the erotic images that sometimes invaded my consciousness were flawed; the pictures swirled and tumbled, went in and out of focus.

Into the dazzling glare of my desire, there came this transformed sister, once again unselfconsciously loving and close. How could I possibly handle it? She was equally provocative and innocent. Still uninhibited, she wore as little as possible around the house, especially on those hot, sticky, sensual days in an age when the only air conditioning was an oscillating electric fan. We played as we had always played. I still made her laugh at the dinner table just as she was drinking a glass of milk. We chased each other around the

the house, wrestled, tickled each other. But now the play moved into a new dimension. Parts of her body drew my hands as if with a powerful magnet. I tickled her a half-second longer than would have been natural. I let my hands move a half-inch closer to her breasts. In the dimension in which I now found myself, another half-second might have meant half a lifetime, another half-inch a passage to an inconceivable paradise.

For her part, Sister was entirely unaffected by incestuous desire. She was not even consciously aware of the changes in my behavior. But her body knew something was up. Deftly, she moved just soon enough and far enough to nullify the extra half-second or half-inch I might have gained. It was an intricate, subtle game of barely perceptible moves and countermoves, played innocently and good-naturedly on her part and equivocally, with a sense of inevitable defeat, on mine. Not once did I consider actually having intercourse with my sister; that was simply beyond my knowledge and imagination. The most I dared imagine (the image would pulse into my mind, disappear, then pulse again) was to see her unclothed or to cup my hands around her breasts. At the height of my insatiable frustration, that image made the erotic imagery of years to come seem pale by comparison.

And there was nothing I could do about it. I became dizzy with desire I couldn't acknowledge. My ears rang with words I couldn't speak. I was so aroused that I was beyond getting an erection. It was the ultimate impotence, the primal tragedy: I would never be able to join with what was closest to me, what I most loved. I knew I had to accept it; what was never seriously considered was not to be.

So I started applying the same kind of mental control I had used at age four to keep from crying when my sister cried. Bored to distraction in school, I flung myself into the big-band world of the late 1930s. I collected records—Goodman, Shaw, Dorsey, Basie. I practiced clarinet for hours along with the records and played alto sax in sleazy pick-up bands, getting slightly high from the marijuana that wafted in my direction from the older saxists on either side of me. At seventeen, I started my own band, modeled ambitiously after my idols Shaw and Goodman, with a full thirteen pieces. After two false starts, everything came together. Sooner than anyone believed possible, we were a spectacular success, with more job offers than we could handle. Not as polished as the leading big band in town, we had a more powerful, driving beat. We played every Count Basie arrangement we could get our hands on. We played the Mary Lou Williams Kansas City Series. We started making our own arrangements. Hearing my only surviving record through the dust and crackle of the decades, you might guess the band to have been composed of free-swinging blacks rather than middle-class whites, ages sixteen through twenty-three.

It was a memorable year. I had more money than I knew what to do with. My pockets were stuffed with five- and ten-dollar bills (Years later, down to my last dollar, I went to the closet and found a wadded-up five-dollar bill in one of the side pockets of my old band jacket.) When the band was only a few months old, I bought a white 1939 Mercury convertible with leather seats. Named the White Roach, my car was also a spectacular success, a winner on the after-hours drag racing scene.

Everything was going my way. And somehow, during the year I was 17, all illicit desire for my sister disappeared. She became a comfortable family member again, my Number One fan, my confidante, my best buddy—nothing more. I erased "the other" from my consciousness. It might never have happened. That feeling and those unacknowledged games might have been only a dream.

My father prospered. We moved to a big house a block from the governor's mansion. We had two little brothers, but they were so much younger that they seemed a second family. Sister entered a fashionable girls' school. With no apparent effort, she made the best grades in her class. She showed me her exam papers. I was awed by her ability to organize facts; in two succinct sentences she would answer a question that would have taken me two pages to answer. She was popular with girls. She joined one of the best sororities. Boys were falling out of trees all around her, but she managed, good humoredly, to keep things in perspective. I was proud and pleased. I felt absolutely no jealousy. In fact, we sometimes double-dated in the White Roach and, at evening's end, necked in the parked car with our respective dates.

Sister was a mature fourteen going on fifteen. She often attended dances where I played. I watched her from the bandstand—a rare flower in white lace-topped, strapless evening dress, gardenias in her hair, her dark eyes sparkling. The dances were extravagant affairs at which boys far outnumbered the girls, and a girl's popularity was measured by the number of breaks she got. I decided to quantify the phenomenon: during one slow chorus of "Moonglow," the band's closing theme, my sister was broken in on thirty times. As far as I know, it was a record. I told all my friends.

Excitement and success in the outside world helped bring things back to "normal." But some great effort had been required to extinguish every flame, every last spark of erotic feeling for my sister. It worked very well indeed. What's not clear is how much that effort cost me.

One Question Remains

The rest is seamless, a story of unflawed love. The year my band was most successful was 1941. That was also the year all of us were to learn we had been living in a dream. The war ripped us out of mythic time, introduced us to history, provided us with a *before* and an *after*: another myth. Still a child, I was soon off for the Air Force. Before the war ended, Sister, not yet quite seventeen, married my best

63

friend. Shortly after the war, I married her best friend. Three sons later for her and two daughters later for me, we got divorced and remarried. This time, my sister didn't know my new wife; but again, her new husband was my closest friend and colleague.

The years have only brought us closer. We have a private saying: "Husbands and wives may come and go, but brothers and sisters are forever." We have told each other things we wouldn't tell anyone else in the world. We have been together at scenes of birth and death and terrible family accidents. Much is unsure in life, but I have one certainty: I know that whenever I need her my sister will come. I know this because it has happened so many times. Two brief episodes from the war demonstrate the point.

After failing a flying test in primary flight school, my spirits hit the depths. Though I didn't ask for a family visit, my voice on the telephone signaled a dire need. The next day, my fearful, nervous mother and sixteen-year-old sister boarded a train bound from Oak Ridge, Tennessee, to Lakeland, Florida. For the better part of two nights and a day, they shared a drafty day coach overflowing with drunken GIs so they could spend a weekend with me, and then returned under the same conditions.

In spite of difficulties, I finished flight school several months later and came home with silver wings and gold bars to Atlanta (my parents had moved back from Oak Ridge) to celebrate my graduation leave. But all my friends had left for the service, and most of the girls I knew were away at college. Two days into my leave, my mother phoned my not-quite-seventeen-year-old sister in Ft. Pierce, Florida, and told her that I "seemed kind of lonely and wasn't having much fun," just that. Sister packed her bags immediately and took the first train to Atlanta. Her husband of less than two weeks, a new navy ensign, was out to sea for the day, so she left word for him with the Red Cross that she was off to spend the next week with her brother.

Who could ever deserve such love? What wife or lover could ever match it?

We are still connected. We see each other almost every week. We phone each other almost every day. I have plotted the direct compass course between her house and mine. She lives just on the other side of Mt. Tamalpais: thirteen winding, hilly miles and four hours by hiking trail, nine miles and twenty-five minutes by street and freeway. Sometimes we give workshops together. She teaches communications skills and women's rights. She often works with groups that are hostile. On one occasion, she spent several days explaining women's rights to Las Vegas firemen, dauntless and joyful as ever, good-naturedly whipping their taunting questions back at them in a way that would leave the questioner speechless and the other firemen chuckling.

Among many recent memories of my sister, one now shines in my consciousness. For two days we had been working with a group of managers from a large corporation. The corporation was under federal investigation for possible discrimination in personnel policies; our workshop was part of their affirmative action program. The managers had been polite but obdurate. More than a two-day workshop was needed (try teams of wild horses) to get equal rights for women and minorities in that tradition-bound group. And yet, when time came for the summation, my sister was as cheerful and unwavering as ever. She told the managers that she had a dream for their corporation, and for them as well. She delivered this potentially melodramatic statement so unpretentiously that they couldn't help but listen. She spoke of the power of the corporation, of the thousands of people it employed, the millions of products it sent out all over the world. She spoke of the need for equal opportunity, not just as a legal expedient or a matter of social justice, but as a means for releasing perhaps surprising human capacities that have languished in their midst.

My sister is over fifty now, but she stands as straight and

confident as she stood, adorned with serpents, at six. Her body is as trim and pleasing to the eye as it was when she danced to the slow beat of "Moonglow" at fourteen. Her voice is clear and compelling. In spite of themselves, the managers were listening.

She spoke of the power of small groups of men and women, even of individuals, to make significant changes in the world. She won't try to press her viewpoint onto them, she said, but only to tell them her own dream. In that dream, each one of them, not just through corporate directives, but through the examples of their own lives—day by day, minute by minute—will act to nourish and further human abilities among employees who happen to be female or black or brown or yellow. My sister is a lovely woman who could probably pass for 35, but the years are beginning to touch her face. I know that time eventually will triumph. Her essence, however, is still the same. She is still the bright-eyed baby I carried around under the watchful eye of our black maid in 1927 in Atlanta, Georgia. There are some things time can never change.

She told the managers (they were extremely quiet) that their example could start a ripple that would spread throughout the corporation. Then the corporation, through its example, could send out ripples that would reach other corporations, bringing them courage to do what the inner heart knows is right. Large-scale shifts in basic attitudes, she said, don't happen overnight. But personal commitment, personal example, can begin tomorrow morning. It can begin, in fact, *right now*.

The managers were hearing her, but some of them had lowered their eyes. My problem was different: sitting there among them, I had to blink to keep tears of love and pride from running down my cheeks. I was not deceiving myself. Some of the managers had been moved by her words. But not very many of them would have transformed their attitudes between that afternoon and the morning. Injustice would probably walk those corporate corridors for some time to come. That was not a happy thought. But I was happy enough right then, happy to the point of tears, in fact, just to be living in the kind of world that had managed to produce someone like my sister.

I also know I have had something few men or women have had: more than fifty years of total, unconditional love.

A question remains: could this love have lasted so many years, could it have been so strong, if somewhere along the way it had achieved erotic fulfillment? Might not there have been a brief interlude, one or two teenage years, when sister and brother could have joined as lovers, with no lasting ill effects? Probably not. Not in this place and time, not in this culture, this world.

More than ever now, I feel we need families that are warm and loving, in which intimacy and physical touch are the rule, not the exception. But each of us probably also needs an oasis where love can be freely expressed and experienced with no worry about eventual seduction or exploitation. Eros is present within the family—there's no question about that —but within that magic circle Eros is constrained. And it is precisely that constraint that forces us into freedom.

What I have learned is that there are no games without rules. Boundaries, bases, and nets intensify the play. Referees are noble guardians of our pleasure, constraining us to play at the highest possible level.

In the game of love, we are confronted by two awesome guardians. One of them, death, is with us always, even when we pretend it is not there, numbering our days, urging us into commitment, into the moment. No matter how many times we say "forever," we know we must eventually say goodbye. What sharper goad to love, to being loving *now*?

We meet the other guardian of the game of love in earliest childhood, when we first awaken to desire. Mysterious, seemingly perverse, this guardian tells us that we must not join with what is closest and sometimes dearest to us. We must begin our erotic quest in frustration and chaos. We must reach out beyond what is familiar and make new worlds of love.

Thus, death and the incest taboo are related. They stand on either side of us, inexorable and unforgiving. Far from diminishing the play, they create the very conditions by which it can transform our lives. If we should ignore either guardian, love would not be nearly so poignant, so rich.

CHAPTER SIX

Face to Face with Eros

I BECAME AWARE of Eros early in life. It was the mysterious force that was more powerful than my powerful father, that drew me toward my beloved sister, that imbued all of nature with an almost painful wonder. The eighth-century B.C. poet, Hesiod, sang of Eros as "the most beautiful of the immortal gods, who in every man and every god softens the sinews and overpowers the prudent purposes of the mind."[1] Dante found Eros in the kind of love that moves the sun and the other stars. Freud saw Eros as an instinct that is continually striving to draw life together into ever-larger entities, thus prolonging life and bringing it into higher development. In this process, according to Freud, Eros works to "combine single human individuals, and after that families, then races, people and nations, into one great unity, the unity of mankind."[2] Freud believed that for the sake of this larger purpose, much sexual energy (one of the expressions of Eros) has to be sublimated, that is, channeled into socially useful activities such as work or artistic creation. In both early and late civilized thought, Eros has been viewed as a powerful and possibly disruptive force, one that calls for constant and vigilant social control.

I have come to see Eros simply as the fundamental creative force in the universe, which manifests itself in the urge within species to reproduce and increase in numbers and in the tendency of life as a whole to evolve (through whatever mechanism, whether biologically or culturally) into higher and more beautifully organized forms. What we now term "sexual desire" is certainly one expression of this force, and so is the broader love that transcends desire. Eros is also expressed in the drive toward friendship and in the desire to join with others in community and common enterprises. For me, as will be seen in chapters 15 and 16, the creative force of Eros is not limited to biological and cultural creation, but extends to every urge to build and create, whether the creation be a bluebird's nest, a new recipe, or a symphony.

In his later writings, Freud found it necessary to balance Eros with an equal and opposite death instinct, which he called Thanatos. This revision of his theory probably stemmed from his own increasing suffering and pessimism as well as from the dualism and mechanism of nineteenth-century science. But I do not believe the dualism is necessary. Death and destruction can be seen as *part of* the creative process. If biological evolution is any indication, death is a skillful and indeed indispensable servant of the creation of higher forms. In human affairs, not death but deadness is the enemy of Eros. Awareness of our mortality heightens love. The denial of death, expressed in unawareness, lassitude, and trivialization, corrupts love.

To engage in "sex" is to follow the urgings of Eros, but only at a distance. One can be obsessed with sex and have only a passing acquaintance with Eros. One can be a sexual high scorer, a master of seduction, and never meet Eros face to face. But sometimes, even in the most loveless life, Eros can suddenly appear, as if out of nowhere, to sweep away every assumption of the past, to turn life upside down.

One man I interviewed, for example, left his first wife, with whom he had felt erotically deprived, and moved into an expensive bachelor apartment, with the express purpose of indulging his sensuality to the full. For the next year and two days, he never spent a night alone. He kept a chart of his sexual encounters, which showed that during those 367 nights he had had sex with exactly fifty different women. Then, on the 368th night, at a meeting of the city planning commission, he felt himself strangely drawn to a woman who was there to oppose the initiative he was supporting.

"When she spoke before the group," he said, "there was something terribly appealing about her, something that touched me very deeply. I talked with her briefly at the end of the first night of the meeting. On the second night, I dozed off, and when I woke up, the first thing I did was look over to see if she was still there.

"I asked her out for a drink. We sat and talked. Everything seemed different. I was on a cloud. I canceled out on the woman I was supposed to meet later that evening. All I wanted to do was to sit and look at Helen. She was conventional, not at all exotic or glamorous, but she changed everything for me. The whole world was different.

"We went away and spent the weekend with friends. I didn't care about sex. All I wanted was to hold her and look into her eyes. We did have sex that weekend, I think, but it was less than successful. As I recall it, I had a sort of premature ejaculation. But that didn't matter. All that mattered was being with her. I just felt that everything was right in the world.

"It was incredible. My perceptions of everything were transformed. The most ordinary things in my life were suddenly extraordinary—the way the sky looked, the trees, the cars passing by. Suddenly, I was in a different world, a different life. As for that year I spent with those fifty women—I'm not knocking it. But it just seemed to fade away. Compared with being in love, it was nothing."

Not long after that, the two were married. They are still together, still in love.

A woman I'll call Sylvia experienced a similar turnaround, but she came to it from a quite different erotic history. Her first sexual experience had been mechanical and physically painful. Then, at college, she had had a long-term affair with a football player she described as "mean." Their sexual encounters were always the same. He would try to overpower her. She would squirm around and fight him off. When he finally prevailed, he would be finished with her in a matter of seconds. He thought it was great. She felt nothing. She did, however, get pregnant, and she almost died from the aftereffects of an abortion. Her response to this nightmarish experience was to move into a singles-type apartment with two other women and, in the spirit of the Sexual Revolution, become totally promiscuous. None of this prepared her for what happened one night when she drove her girlfriend out to a beach house to see her lover.

"There was another man there I'd known before, but not sexually. His name was Tom. It was a beautiful Indian Summer night. The stars were out, and maybe the dance of the ocean had something to do with it. Anyway, I ended up spending the night. Tom and I were in one of the bedrooms, in separate beds. Then he said, 'Why don't you come over to my bed?'

"It was magical. Up until then, I'd always tried to please a man, to try and figure out what he wanted, knowing I'd feel nothing. But something happened—I don't know what—and this time it was totally different. We spent hours just touching, touching each other all over. The orientation was not sex. It was being together. When we finally made love, it was very slow and beautiful, a religious experience. Our bodies truly became one. No talk was needed. We were pure energy. There was no thought of orgasm. My whole body was in orgasm all the time. I imagine my fingertips had as much orgasm as my vagina. Everything was joined. It was beyond all words.

"The next morning, when we saw each other on the beach, we couldn't speak. We were almost afraid to look at each other, it had been so powerful and beautiful. After that, we slowly developed a relationship. But we didn't make love again for three or four months. The first night had been sacred. That's why we didn't talk about it and didn't make love again for so long."

After a relationship of nearly five years, Sylvia became pregnant. She wanted the baby. Tom didn't. She got an abortion, and the two of them drifted apart. But the power of that first night still serves as a weather vane for her life, her hopes for the future.

"What I got was myself," Sylvia said. "I didn't hold anything back, and I got myself."

I, too, have had my feet swept from under me and have had my life transformed by love. I have also followed Eros up some blind alleys and on occasion have emerged severely chastened. But through all of this, through all of my life, I have always wanted to see Eros face to face. I have wished above almost all wishes to move my life in rhythm with this most powerful of forces, not just during the rare, magical moments, but on a daily basis, all the time.

I am not a connoisseur of disembodied love. While I can admire that transmutation of physical love into philosophical "love of beauty" so eloquently proposed by Socrates in the *Symposium*, the love I have always sought is ultimately full-bodied. For me, the erotic force that vibrates throughout all of nature has its finest human expression in the joining of bodies along with hearts, minds, and spirits. Through that joining, I have entered into states that can only be called religious. I have experienced alterations of perception, of time and space. I have sensed that absolute unity so celebrated in the literature of erotic love, a sense of oneness that extends not only to my lover but also to the larger world. But of all my intimate meetings with Eros, the one I have chosen to describe here is the most improbable, most unexpected, and most difficult to tell.

The time was the summer of 1965, and it seemed to some of us that Eros was on the loose in American society as never before, promising the breakdown of age-old oppressiveness in matters of race, sexuality, education, and human relations, along with the creation of new kinds of communities and perhaps of a more elegantly organized society. It was a happy if somewhat naive interlude in a troubled decade when very little in the way of positive reform seemed entirely impossible. I had just made a new friend, a young man of extraordinary brilliance, charm, and creativity. My new friend had a keen sense of history and an immense store of knowledge about both Western and Eastern philosophy. We talked for hours on end. We dreamed up scenarios of large-scale social transformation. During one of our talks, I asked him if he believed in the existence of a personal god.

"God is *at least* personal."

He went on to explain that according to Eastern thought and Christian mysticism as well there is an essential ground of all being that has a personal aspect and also is more than personal. Because he had experienced this essential ground directly during extended periods of meditation, my friend was certain it existed. I asked him how I could gain such a sense of certainty. He hesitated, then told me that a number of philosophers and religious leaders were currently using the drug LSD in their quest for religious understanding and that he knew a psychologist who could lead me and my wife, Lillie, on such a quest if we so desired. Hesitantly, I told him I would like to try it and Lillie probably would too.

Two nights later, I received a phone call from the psychologist, who introduced himself and said, "I hear you're interested in taking a trip." I had never before heard the word "trip" used in that context and was immediately filled with a sense of adventure, of imminent departure on a journey of some magnitude. The psychologist laid out the conditions for the journey. He would come to our house at three in the afternoon on the appointed day. He would be accompanied by his female assistant so that what he termed the feminine principle as well as the masculine principle would be represented in any mythic material that might come up. My wife and I would agree not to leave our premises at any time during the experience. We would lodge our children elsewhere from no later than noon on the day of the session until at least noon the following day. We would arrange to be calm and silent for at least two hours before the psychologist and his assistant arrived.

On the day of the trip, we drove our two daughters, aged five and one, to my sister's house. We came home and waited, in silence and not without a few fine thrills of apprehension, for the arrival of our guides.

At this point in my story, I am overcome with the urge to make all sorts of disclaimers: that LSD was not an illegal substance in 1965; that the promiscuous, recreational use of the drug (which was to parallel the promiscuous use of sexual freedom) had not yet become a problem; that my wife and I were on a responsible quest. But these vain disclaimers are secondary to a more serious concern. I know that there are many people—and I don't entirely exclude myself—who tend to dismiss any experience that occurs under the influence of a chemical substance, especially one as powerful and dangerous as LSD. Isn't it true, one might ask, that the main effect of the drug is simply to disorient and confuse? This is partially true. According to the best thinking on the subject, LSD interferes temporarily with the feedback circuits in the nervous system that maintain the normal homeostasis of perception and consciousness. This can be terrifying to a young person who, with no preparation or guidance, pops a pill and goes to the amusement park. It can be utterly devastating to someone who is given the drug without his or her own knowledge—as was the case in a number of covert, government-sponsored experiments that have only recently come to light.

But for one who is well-prepared and guided and who

has a sincere purpose, the very characteristics of the drug that can cause terror and devastation can be turned to an advantage; for LSD is particularly effective in cutting off the circuits of cultural conditioning that might be necessary for everyday life but prevent the perception of a perhaps wider and more fundamental reality. "If the doors of perception were cleansed," William Blake wrote, "everything would be seen as it is, infinite." The sincere purpose of those who experimented with LSD in a philosophical and religious context was to cleanse, not cloud, the doors of perception. It is easy to overlook the fact that the material that comes up in an LSD experience is altogether a product of the perceptions and consciousness of the person involved, not something "implanted" by the drug. In my own case, I could discover, finally, no good reason for dismissing what I saw and what I learned.

The psychologist arrived with a stack of classical records. He looked like a college psych prof. He was accompanied by a soft-spoken young woman with long, straight black hair. After a talk on our responsibilities, the psychologist gave us two plain white pills. Lillie and I looked at each other with the smiles of parachutists about to step out of an airplane, and swallowed them.

For the next fifteen or twenty minutes, we sat quietly, enjoying the mild euphoria of those who have willingly taken a fateful and irreversible step. Then I began getting occasional flashes of ecstasy along with deeper twinges of anxiety. Lillie reported that she felt thousands of champagne bubbles lifting her arms and shoulders. The psychologist seemed unduly preoccupied with the records. The one that was playing seemed extremely scratchy. He removed it and began rubbing it around and around with an electrostatic record cleaning pad. How annoying! It seemed he would never stop cleaning the record. At last he put it back on the stereo. It seemed scratchier than ever.

By this time, I could hardly bear to sit still. I squirmed

from one position to another but could find no comfort or ease. I tried walking back and forth, but that didn't help. Lillie went over and lay on the cushioned window seat before the bay windows at the front of the room. I lay in the middle of the living room rug, sweating all over, feeling as uneasy as it was possible to feel. Again and again, I tried to get control of myself. Each effort at control made things worse. I began to understand my situation: I was going to have to relinquish all control. There was no alternative, no other way out.

This knowledge terrified me. Since earliest childhood, I had learned in countless ways—from my father, from my Southern white culture, from flying combat missions in the South Pacfiic—that a male must always maintain control. To give up control would be, for me, like dying. Premonitions of another reality were beginning to intrude on my consciousness. In this new reality, each of the four of us in the room knew what the others were thinking. The intrusion was anything but gentle. The new reality was thrusting itself into me crudely and with great force. It was the reality, I thought, of a schizophrenic. The psychologist and the young woman were busy with Lillie at the window seat. She was obviously farther along than I was—more adventurous, less constrained by the need for control.

How long was this terrible unease going to last? Now the psychologist was cleaning another record, scrubbing it so hard it seemed he might go right through it. "I need help," I thought. "I wish he would come over here." With my unspoken words, he turned and walked over. *Of course!* He kneeled and leaned down over me, his face kindly.

"What's the trouble?" he asked.

"You know," I answered, convinced he could read my mind.

"Yes, but tell me anyway."

"I'm afraid," I said, trembling all over.

"What are you afraid of?"

"You know," I whispered.

"Tell me anyway."

I waited for what seemed a long time, afraid to say it, ashamed to lose control. I tried one more time to think of some other way out. There was no other way. At last I said it softly but clearly.

"Death. I'm afraid of death."

With those words, the world stopped. Just as action is frozen on a movie or television screen, everything in the room stood stock-still. And the face that was frozen above me was a ghastly green. I turned as cold as ice. The psychologist had become a cadaver. He was death. I wanted to turn away, but I knew I had no real choice except to look at him, at death, full in the face. I looked, and instead of fear, I experienced release. Everything let go. My self-control was gone. "Manliness" was simply irrelevant. I burst into tears. I sobbed and wailed without shame or any other consideration. And with this release, this giving up, I found myself in another reality.

I am aware at this point of the difficulty, if not the folly, of attempting to describe an alternate reality in the language of our everyday reality. The difficulty in this case is compounded by the fact that on the surface nothing at all had changed. Everything in the living room was just the same as before. There was Lillie on the window seat at the large bay windows. Our guides were sitting nearby on the rug, watching me with great compassion. And there, just as before, were the chairs and the couch, record player, lamps, tables, fireplace. Everything was exactly the same, *but much, much more so*. I looked at one of my chairs as if I had never seen a chair before. Here was the ultimate chair, the Platonic idea of a chair. Far from being blurred or confused, all the objects of my daily life were startlingly clear and unequivocal, so *real* that I could hardly bear to look at them. The room resounded with incredible vitality, power, and meaningfulness. I knew what it was like to be fully alive and awake. I had turned my eyes from the flickering images on the wall of the cave. At last, I was seeing the world in the clear white light of day, as it really was.

As for the music, the static was completely gone, and every note was brilliant and immediate. The room was not big enough to hold it. A horn call on the stereo seemed to emerge from our bedroom three rooms away. Yes, the horns were clearly there, enormous gleaming golden horns many times more powerful and resonant than the instruments we now know, not so much frightening as fateful: hunters' horns, calling to me from our bedroom at the back of the house. I had an urge to cry out to the psychologist, "Why didn't you *tell* me it was going to be like this?" Then I realized he couldn't possibly have told me, since there are no words for it.

But these attempts at description, these futile words, can easily become tedious. The "ground of being" was my hoped-for destination on this journey, and something was still missing. I looked over at Lillie. She was lying on her back on the window seat holding a red rose in her hand, now and then smelling it. I wanted her to come to me. With the thought (*again!*) she got up and started walking over to where I was lying on the rug. She opened her arms and came to me in slow motion. It seemed to take a long time, bringing to mind those sentimental and archetypal commercials on television in which a beautiful woman holding a flower runs in slow motion through high grasses toward the viewer. It was like that, except that Lillie seemed infinitely more beautiful, her face as supernaturally white and pure as the imagined faces of those thirteenth-century ladies of whom the minstrels sang. She fell into my arms and my tears literally overflowed. I cried with relief that I would no longer have to hold anything back. I cried for our every misunderstanding, every lost opportunity to love each other. I cried for the foolhardy bravery of what we were attempting just by being married and having children. We had come together seven years earlier with the passionate certainty of the young. The birth of our first daughter had brought joy and an inexplicable change in our relationship. Our intensity became dissonant. Our passion turned to bewilderment. Our bewilderment became a complex contest over sex. Now all of this seemed unimportant. Something larger was beckoning me.

After what seemed a very long time, the tears stopped and I lay in absolute silence and clarity. The music was Rodrigo's haunting *Concierto de Aranjuez*, and I was that music. Lillie and I lay on the rug next to each other. She handed me the rose. I held it for a few moments, then gave it back to her. This simple interchange seemed immensely significant to me. I closed my eyes and found myself in some other kind of time and place. Something was drawing me downward into the vortex of a powerful, primal experience, which I recognized immediately as the act of love. There were no pictures of this act, or any sensation of passion, but rather the feeling of an inexorable force. It was like experiencing the silent impulse that underlies music, or the essential, nonmaterial relationship of forces that makes a suspension bridge possible. I realized that the underlying structure of the act of love was infinitely more powerful than the act itself, that it could ultimately destroy anything that got in its way.

Shaken, I returned at last to my living room and reached over for the rose that Lillie was holding. When she gave it to me with a beatific smile, I was grateful and reassured. I gave it back and went away again, now for a much longer journey. It seemed on this journey that I could somehow reenact the meeting and joining of countless lovers of many and varied cultures and historical periods, not the physical manifestation of love and lust, but the deeper, underlying structure. And now somehow Lillie was part of the experience, involved with me and with the experience of ancient lovers—reenacting the experience, *becoming* it. I was away so long on this journey that I began suffering all the poignant, bittersweet longings of homesickness. I returned and reached for the rose. That it was still there seemed a miracle and a validation as well, a symbol of our connection, a tiny lifeline to the familiar three-dimensional world of matter and energy, time and space.

This process continued for some two hours, which for me were entirely outside of ordinary time. With each exploration I relinquished more and more of the appurtenances of ordinary life, which might be said to include sight, hearing, and all other sensory input, language, ego, maleness, time, space, gravity, mass, even the sense of having a separate body. With each giving up, I came closer to the irreducible heart of existence, closer to the essential ground I had been seeking. I have no idea how many times I brought myself back to the room to exchange the rose with Lillie. But in the end, as we were to discover, nothing remained of it but a two-inch-long fragment of the stem, polished to a fine gloss by having been passed from hand to hand so many times.

And what was left when all that was unessential had been discarded? For me, there was still a sense of *I-ness*, of a personal identity that could somehow survive every possible loss. There was, as well, a sense of unity, of all existence as a single, ultimately indivisible entity. And underlying this paradox, making up the essential ground, recreating it every instant, was Eros: a fiercely burning erotic force which—relentlessly, at all costs—would go on forever creating form out of chaos. What my friend had offered I had discovered inadvertently with Lillie. At the heart of existence was love.

The effects of the drug gradually wore off. Lillie and I helped each other up. We hadn't noticed that night had come. The room had returned to its former dimensions. The electric lights dazzled. We walked around regaining our balance. Our guides were all smiles. We ordered a large Chinese dinner. It was wonderful to be there drinking beer and eating Chinese food after having traveled so long out in the winds of eternity. I told my story with great enthusiasm. All along, I assumed that Lillie had in some way shared my travels. After all, we had the polished stem of the rose as proof of our connectedness.

But Lillie had a different story. She had been aware, she said, that I very much wanted her with me, and she had quickly realized the importance of the rose. But passing it back and forth every few seconds was quite distracting. With all her heart, she said, she wanted to be available to me. At the same time, she was eager to embark on her own exploration.

"So I got ready to leave my body," she explained, "though I had no idea how that might happen. But first I wanted everything to be right for you. I made sure my body was warm and a smile was on my face. Suddenly, I was looking down on the two of us as we lay on the living room floor. You seemed fine, so I knew I could leave. Instantly, I was in outer space, moving just as if I were under water. I could see all the brilliant galaxies and in one corner the Earth, also brightly lit. I was comfortably at home, swimming in the universe. Then I realized that I and the cosmos were actually located inside my head. All of that, the whole universe, was there—enough space so that I knew I could never again feel crowded or pushed into a corner.

"Coming down I saw some kind of structure. It had seventeen levels and each of the levels was performing a separate function. I realized those seventeen levels were parts of my personality and that they weren't integrated. It was funny. I laughed to myself at the rightness of it. Then each of the levels, one by one, came down onto my body. Each one fit perfectly, like a layer of skin, putting me back together again. As each layer landed, I said, 'There comes another one.'"

I experienced a pang of disappointment and a short, swift fall into what we call "objective reality"—that useful, disillusioned state in which discourse is limited to those things we can measure and generally agree upon. Some of the wonder was dimmed, but we had lived long enough in the twentieth-century to accept the idea of multiple realities. Both stories had their truth to tell, and each in its own way was valid; my encounter with Eros continued to resonate in my consciousness. Instead of a miracle, we had the dubious rewards of irony: our diverging paths on that journey made a good story to tell our friends.

To wrap up this episode, two more things need to be said. Lillie and I missed few of the challenges offered in this age to married people with children. We raised our daughters. We had stormy days and sunny, many adventures, and not one boring moment. But our paths continued to diverge, and we finally parted.

As for LSD, I never had a desire to take it again. The years have shown me that it is possible to meet Eros face to face simply in the act of giving yourself totally to your lover, or even in the daily process of living wholeheartedly, in full awareness of the present moment. For Eros is by no means an exotic stranger, but rather a constant companion, unperceived and unacknowledged only to the extent that we are careless, forgetful of our own existence.

When the samurai Kikushi was ordained a *bodhisattva*, his master told him, "You must concentrate upon and consecrate yourself wholly to each day, as though a fire were raging in your hair." To live and love in such a manner is not easy in this culture, for we are continually seduced by comforts, goodies, and conveniences, the drone of "entertainment," the distraction of "sex." But Eros is always with us, ready at any moment to light a fire in our hair, to transform our lives.

PART III

Eros Betrayed

CHAPTER SEVEN

Love Is a Different Matter

Lenina shook her head. "Somehow," she mused, "I haven't been feeling very keen on promiscuity lately. There are times when one doesn't. Haven't you found that too, Fanny?"

Fanny nodded her sympathy and understanding. "But one's got to make the effort," she said sententiously, "one's got to play the game. After all, every one belongs to every one else."

"Yes, every one belongs to every one else," Lenina repeated slowly and, sighing, was silent for a moment: then, taking Fanny's hand, gave it a little squeeze. "You're quite right, Fanny. As usual. I'll make the effort."

Aldous Huxley,
Brave New World

In HUXLEY's brilliant anti-utopian novel, promiscuity is compulsory (children are taught sex-play from infancy on), and *love* is a dirty word. America of the 1980s is not yet Huxley's brave new world, but recent decades have obviously moved us in that direction. Today, there are men and women who can talk about their most intimate sexual behavior as if they are describing a stroll in the park, then become flustered and embarrassed at the mention of love. In an article called "Welcome to the Modern World," the April 1981 *Esquire* uses the words of photographer Marcus Leatherdale, "a chronicler of the urban hip," to sum up the "modern" attitude on this matter:

"No responsibility, no commitment, everything for the moment, rely on no one but yourself—I don't think it's natural. And the biggest mistake of all is to let anyone know you're in love with them. Then they feel cornered. There's just no room for romance in the modern world." He smiled a grim smile. "It's as cold and hard as the graphics."

Esquire at least broaches the subject of love, which is more than can be said for most current writing on sexuality. It is strange indeed to read one authoritative sex book after another and find love treated only in passing or not at all. A case in point is *The Sex Atlas*, by Erwin J. Haeberle, not a shabby effort but rather one of the best of its kind. It is scholarly yet readable, up-to-date yet historically informed.[1] In 509 pages, it treats everything from "Painful Intercourse in Men" to " 'Natural Law' and the Laws of Nature." But, as in many modern books on sex, precious few are the mentions of love, and those that do slip in are historical and faintly pejorative. We are told, for example, that in Freud's time sex, love, marriage, and procreation were considered inseperable and that sex without love was considered evil. We are introduced to various attitudes toward love in other cultures. We are offered the view that the modern nuclear family has no function beyond providing love and intimacy, which is "by no means enough to justify its existence." And that's about it for love. Five-hundred-and-nine pages.

The author of *The Sex Atlas* is a faculty member at the Institute for Advanced Study of Human Sexuality, a unique professional graduate school that offers four graduate degree programs in the field of sexology. The Institute is housed in an unobtrusive two-story building on a heavily traveled one-way street not far from San Francisco's fashionable Pacific Heights district. Inside are not only offices and classrooms but also a hot tub and massage tables, a bookstore with a department for vibrators, a library, and a superb collection of erotic films and tapes. The National Sex Forum also operates out of the same building, with most of the same people, to provide counseling and sex education for professionals and nonprofessionals.

The Forum's most famous offering—it has been attended by more than 50,000 people since 1968—is a fifteen-hour introductory course called Human Sexuality #101. The course is given once a month, and is attended mostly by fledgling sex therapists, members of other human services professions, and nonprofessionals who have been sent by their own counselors. It begins at 1 P.M. on Saturday, breaks for dinner at 6 P.M., reconvenes at 8 P.M., and ends two hours later. On Sunday, the course starts at 10 A.M. and ends at 6 P.M., with an hour-and-a-half lunch break at noon. All the sessions are held in a spacious, two-story-high "multi-media-room." At the back of the room are carpeted tiers furnished with oversized cushions on which up to forty people can lounge while the program unfolds: lectures, panel discussions, and, more than anything else, films and slides projected on the high wall at the front of the room.

Human Sexuality #101 is based on a process that the Forum calls Sexual Attitude Restructuring (SAR). The basic idea is to offer a certain amount of useful sex information; to break down stereotypes and misconceptions about homosexuals, bisexuals, the aging, and the handicapped; to desensitize members of the audience so that they won't be shocked by a wide variety of sexual behavior; and to present sex as a rich and enjoyable experience.

In terms of these goals, the course I attended as part of my research for this book worked very well indeed, not only for me but also for other participants with whom I talked. There were a few particularly illuminating moments. For instance, our male sexuality panel was made up of three men. We were told at the beginning that one was straight, one gay, and one bisexual—but we were not told which was which. After a short period of general discussion by the panelists, we were given the opportunity to identify them by sexual preference and to give the reasons for our choices.

Several of us tried. No one got all three identifications right. So much for that set of stereotypes.

The films, generally shown two to four at a time, dominate the program. Most are the work of Dr. Laird Sutton, a Methodist minister turned erotic filmmaker. Sutton's films have little in common with commercial pornography. They attempt to portray sex as natural, fun, sometimes funny, always esthetically pleasing. The cumulative effect was overwhelming.

At one point, after what seemed like hundreds of filmed couplings over a period of several hours, there came a moment when the four images on the wall were of a gay couple, a straight couple, a lesbian couple, and a bisexual group. The subjects were nude and the camera angles in all four frames were such that no sexual organs were visible. I felt myself becoming disoriented. Was that a woman beneath that man whose pelvis was moving so urgently—or another man? And that woman in the second frame from the right—was she kissing a man or a woman? I struggled to force the acts I was watching into their proper boxes. Our group leader had named the four categories before showing the films, and now I couldn't remember which was which. Wasn't I *supposed* to make these discriminations? I searched for clues. There were none. I began to feel uncomfortable.

Soon I realized that to avoid vertigo and nausea I would have to give up the attempt to discriminate and simply surrender to the experience. I didn't really have to know which was which. In all four cases, whoever and whatever was involved, the essential gestures, facial expressions, sounds, pelvic movements, and rhythms were the same. Here were human beings responding to a common human urge, enjoying themselves, giving enjoyment to others. The differences, for which lives have been ruined, were now not only trivial but invisible.

Sensory overload reached its climax on Saturday night with a multimedia event called the Fuckorama. As we lounged on cushions in the darkness, the whole wall lit up with images of human beings and sometimes animals engaging in every conceivable sexual act, accompanied by wails, squeals, moans, shouts, and the first movement of the Tchaikovsky violin concerto. It was a technical triumph: up to seventeen simultaneous moving pictures, mostly excerpted from commercial pornography, projected over a period of forty minutes. How did we react? There was shock, laughter, sporadic arousal, and, finally, boredom. By the end of the Fuckorama, nothing seemed shocking. The physical act of sexual joining seemed commonplace. I considered myself thoroughly desensitized.

On Sunday afternoon, near the end of the course, the subject was sex among the handicapped. As usual, there were numerous films, interspersed with visits by people in wheelchairs. Any of us who might have been dulled and drained by too much explicit sex were quickly revivified by one of the visitors. She was a young female lawyer who also happened to be a paraplegic. Such was the strength of her personality and the radiance of her presence that, from the moment she wheeled herself into the room accompanied by her unhandicapped boyfriend, she had our hearts in her hands. She told us of the despair that had followed the automobile accident that had left her paralyzed in her teens and of what it was like to discover that she could still have a rich, satisfying sex life. She explained that sexual arousal, being mediated by the flow of hormones through her bloodstream, can take place in a paralyzed person even in the absence of muscular control and specific genital sensation; during and after sex, there is a general suffusion of warmth and satisfaction. What's more, parts of the body that aren't paralyzed can become highly sensitized. In her case, orgasm is possible just through the stimulation of her breasts. Her boyfriend provided expert witness on all that she had to say, and she made her case handily: handicapped people want, need, and can have sex, too.

But we didn't require much convincing. The courage and dash of the handicapped people in the films was truly inspiring. The best moment of the weekend for me occurred in one of Laird Sutton's films. A nude woman is shown sitting in the middle of a bed waiting for her paraplegic boyfriend. We see him wheeling toward the bed at full tilt. When the wheelchair strikes the side of the bed, he propels himself onto the mattress in an exuberant forward flip and starts taking off his clothes.

I left Human Sexuality #101 with at least a glimpse at the world that the National Sex Forum envisages: a world in which sex information is readily available for everyone, in which sexual prejudice is non-existent, and in which people have sex whenever they wish, with whomever they wish, and however they wish, just so long as their actions are non-exploitative, conscious, and mutual. Not a bad world, especially for the millions of people who still suffer the agonies of sexual ignorance, deprivation and prejudice.

But as I drove home, I began to get a slightly uneasy feeling. It was almost as if I had been conned, not by the course (it was straightforward enough), but by my own conditioned response to take the most liberated position, to be impeccably nonjudgmental, whatever my deeper feelings. My ambivalence fastened on the fact that love had not been mentioned once during the entire weekend. I brought this up later in an interview with Maggie Rubenstein, who had been our leader in Human Sexuality #101. Dr. Rubenstein is a tall, erect, chic woman in her forties, charming yet somewhat severe in aspect. She is the mother of two teenage children. She could pass for the headmistress of an exclusive girls' school. She is an avowed bisexual and sexual radical.

"Human Sexuality 101 is about sex," she explained. "It's not about love or romance or intimacy. There are other workshops that deal with those subjects. We want to work on the stuff that's hard to talk about. If we spread ourselves around, we couldn't focus right on sex. Love is a different matter. I love my friend, my dog, my fish.

"I tend to be pretty down-to-earth about relationships. I think the romantic ideal can sometimes get in the way of seeing each other as independent beings. I know some people who can never do anything without each other. Love can be limiting. Some people say, 'Because I love you and you love me, you've got to go to bed with me, only me, and do it the way I want.' But love isn't necessary for pleasure. There can also be lustful sex that's good. Let's acknowledge there's love out there. But let's deal with sex."

"During the weekend," I said, "you often used the phrase 'getting it on'. Just what did you mean by that?"

She smiled. " 'Getting it on' is anything that's intimate and shared and sensual."

Dr. Rubenstein is forthright and clear in her sexual radicalism. "The next twenty years are going to be rough, with a backlash against the gains we've made. ERA is in trouble. Gay Rights is in trouble. But I'm an incurable optimist. We'll probably see some pockets of sanity. Children and old people will be less exploited. We'll have better pornography. We might see television become the medium it could be in the area of sexual freedom. Already some important questions on sexuality have been raised in the popular magazines, such as *People*. You can't put the genie back in the bottle. I like *Playboy*. I also like *Hustler*. Rednecks need good sex education too. I'm totally against censorship of all types."

Maggie Rubenstein's colleague, the Reverend Ted McIlvenna, head of the Institute and Forum, is equally forthright. "Pornographic films," he said, "have done more to help people see their options than all the sex therapists in town."

Like Laird Sutton, with whom he has co-authored a book,[2] Dr. McIlvenna is a Methodist minister. He is a heavyset man with the face and physique of a boxer who has let himself get out of shape. On the occasion of our first interview, he received me from a hot tub, in the style of a Roman emperor. As we talked, I was impressed with his concern for freedom of information about sex. Accurate information, he felt, would clear up most sexual problems. He also seemed to be saying that if sex is good, even more sex is better.

"We're now studying supernormal, self-actualized people

in the area of their own sexuality—the Sexually Healthy Person. We're finding that these people have a different view of sex than ordinary people. They've had more exposure to sexual material, have seen more sex movies, have had more fantasies. They're also more liberal in other areas of life. They've read more about sex, thought more about it, and had more sex partners.

"One thing we've learned is that if you're going to have a good sex life you're going to have to work at it. It's a matter of spending more time and effort to get back more reward. People who masturbate the most have the best sex life.

"I have a Game Kit I take with me whenever I go on a trip. This has to do with planning ahead for my own pleasure. It's all set up—several vibrators, artificial penises, French ticklers, leather sheets and massage oil, ostrich feathers, tape recorders with sounds, erotic books and magazines, and some game books on sexual fantasies."

It seemed useless at this point to ask why love was not mentioned in Human Sexuality #101. Something called "sex" loomed so large that it blotted out everything else. And the larger it loomed the less significant it seemed. I recalled that by the end of the Fuckorama I could honestly testify that nothing about sex was shocking. But nothing was sacred either.

In *The Sex Atlas*, Erwin Haeberle offers his own proposal for liberation, a "new morality" for the future: "Today, we need to encourage not only procreational but also recreational sex." According to Haeberle, "once we accept recreation as a legitimate purpose of sex, many of our traditional moral standards, criminal laws, and psychiatric assumptions no longer make sense." If sex is to be enjoyed for its own sake, Haeberle says, "contraception will have to be made available to everyone from the age of puberty, and the old taboos against advertising contraceptives on radio, television, or billboards will have to fall."

There is no need here to spell out all possible implications of a future "recreative" sexual morality. In the present context it is enough if we realize that some drastic changes are likely and that, even in the sexual sphere, we may eventually have to "think the unthinkable."[3]

Haeberle cites population control through total sexual freedom as one such previously unthinkable possibility.

This new morality would indeed cause drastic changes in our social and spiritual life. But we don't have to wait for the year 2000 to witness the advent of recreative sex. We have already seen the transforming process of erotic arousal becoming as casual (sometimes as obligatory) as a goodnight kiss. Millions of people already are engaged in "sex" with "no responsibility, no commitment, everything for the moment," barely able to remember their most recent partner's name or face, some of them arriving at singles' bars after work on Fridays packed and ready for an out-of-town weekend, having no idea with whom they'll spend the next two nights. It's now possible, in fact, to buy a small "One-Nighter's Kit," containing disposable toilet articles and other recreational necessities. Haeberle's new morality is hardly futuristic.

Some sexologists, especially those associated with the universities, are critical of the National Sex Forum for its flamboyance and its refusal to soften its message by using academic language. To the contrary, I admired the Forum revolutionaries precisely because they insisted on being candid, uncompromising, and clear. Nor could I finally question their flamboyant discourse or their multimedia shock tactics; such extreme measures might well be needed to overcome the equally extreme sexual ignorance, prejudice, fear, and guilt that still remain from our Victorian past.

It was even understandable, in a specialized society, that sex would be treated as a specialized activity, existing apart from love and creation, from the society and the cosmos.

But in this, finally, I saw something insidious: a tendency (by no means limited to sexology) to fragment all of life into abstract compartments, the better to study and dominate it, leading at worst to dehumanization, trivialization, and a sort of deadness. I tried to think of sex as separate from the rest of my existence and failed. I wanted to cry out to the sexologists that they had met the challenge of revolution but not of transformation, that the larger challenge lay in not disconnecting the erotic from the rest of life but rather in revealing the intricate, inescapable connections.

CHAPTER EIGHT

Disconnections

To the extent that any culture abstracts and generalizes the erotic, disconnecting it from the rest of life, and depersonalizes the act of love, it has moved toward the ultimate acceptance of genocide and nuclear holocaust.

This statement might seem extreme, but do not leave it without considering the fact that it is easier to contemplate the possible death of 100 million people—if those deaths are treated abstractly in some sort of "study" as "casualties"— than to contemplate the possible death of one person who is a friend, lover, family member, or even acquaintance. Wherever human beings are treated abstractly, in general categories, one of the chief preconditions for genocide has been realized. Wherever anything as intrinsically intimate as erotic relations become depersonalized and disconnected, a large step toward that precondition has been taken.

The disconnections of our time can be clearly seen in our current preoccupation with "sex," which is itself a historical curiosity. The term "human sexual behavior," as *The Sex Atlas* points out, was unknown until fairly recent times, and the very idea that something called "sex" could be perceived, experienced, and studied as being distinct from the rest of life would have been incomprehensible to people of earlier centuries.

During 99 percent of the time that human beings have lived on earth, they have lived in small bands as hunters and gatherers. It is possible both to denigrate and to romanticize this primitive form of life, but it is impossible to deny its *wholeness*. The band itself served all the functions of such institutions as schools, courts, and governments. No social classes or specialized occupations (with the exception of part-time shamans and hunting leaders) fragmented the fabric of primitive life. There was no sense of history, only "the creation" followed by continual social equilibrium. Social relations, as anthropologist Elman R. Service points out, were interpersonal rather than status oriented; adults were not alienated from their society but participated in every aspect of it.[1] Nature was not separate from man and woman. Art, religion, and the erotic were interwoven. Every act— weaving a basket, killing a deer, making love—was essentially sacramental.

We can see in such surviving cultures as the Pygmies of Africa, the Arapesh of New Guinea and the Lepchas of Sikkim that primitive people are well aware that men and women have different primary sexual characteristics: a source of endless merriment among them. There are, as well, certain primitive customs and taboos in areas we now would call "sexual." But all this is simply a part of life, not something to be isolated in a "field" called "sex."

In our own civilization, the word *sexus* was an invention of the Romans, who probably derived it from the Latin verb *secare*, "to cut or sever." For centuries, this word referred only to gender. The same is true of the English noun "sex," which probably first appeared in a 1382 translation from the Latin Bible to describe Noah's selection of "the maal sex and femaal" of each animal. Here the word meant nothing more than gender or type. It was only in the eighteenth-century that the noun "sex" and the adjective "sexual" broadened in definition to include reproduction as well as gender.

It was about this time, in fact, that the Western intellect was achieving the first great successes in the modern campaign to dominate the natural world through classification, generalization, and the creation of a grand realm of abstract, Newtonian relationships. Nothing, not even the erotic, was to escape the advance of purposive rationality, and the newly minted word "sexual" was used in more and more generalizations. We can see this in the *Oxford English Dictionary* listing of the entry dates of various sexual terms into the printed language: "sexual function" (1803), "sexual organs" (1828), "sexual desire" (1836), "sexual instinct" (1861), "sexual impulse" (1863), "sexual act"(1888), and "sexual immorality" (1911). A similar progression exists in other European languages.

Love, desire, longing, and lust have always existed, but it was only under the repressive Victorians, ironically, that "sex" as a separate, highly charged entity really came into its own. In the very act of constraining erotic expression, the Victorians extracted sex from the matrix of social relations, made it lurid, then held it up to view as something alien, an abstraction. During Victoria's reign, as French philosopher Michel Foucault has pointed out, "Sex was driven out of hiding and forced to lead a discursive life."[2] We are still engaged in that discourse, and indeed it might be said that the modern Sexual Revolution is essentially a continuation of Victorian dynamics. Prescription has replaced proscription, liberation has replaced repression, but the preoccupation and the context in which the preoccupation occurs remains the same: "sex" as a well-defined, highly charged entity that dominates much of our thoughts, feelings, and actions.

"Human sexuality" does not exist in nature. It is an abstraction, an idea. The idea obviously fills certain modern needs, or it would not have emerged and survived. But such abstractions can mislead as well as inform. We can come to assume, for example, that our erotic life exists apart from the rest of our life, which is far from the truth. We can choose to believe that our sexual problems and disappointments require sexual solutions, which is often not at all the case. Today, this idea, this abstraction, has taken on bizarre dimensions. "Human sexuality" is so broad that it can include the ERA, the relationship of Tristan and Iseult, and a rape in Central Park under a single heading. At the same time, it is so narrow that it can almost entirely exclude love, empathy, compassion, morality, and creation. Furthermore, the abstraction and generalization involved in our modern way of thinking about sex takes erotic experience, which thrives only in the ever-changing interplay between the unique and the universal, and freezes it in perceptual concrete. To this extent, "human sexuality" serves not aliveness but deadness, and ultimately not life but death.

Depersonalization and Mass Murder

The power of the abstracting, generalizing intellect is well established. This mode of thought has helped us organize society, to control matter and energy, to create useful new fields of endeavor. The flaws and dangers are perhaps less well understood. We tend to forget that nature does not abstract or generalize. The color "green," for example, is an abstraction, and a relatively recent one. Primitive hunters and gatherers have no such concept, not because their color sense is less sophisticated but because their ecological sense is far more sophisticated than ours. They simply can't afford the sloppiness of the generalization "green," for they deal in a world of finer distinctions. Once the perception is firmly locked into "green," a particular bush can never again be quite so vivid and unique as to its particular color. In the same way, the generalization "brown" does nothing to help the hunter distinguish the stag from the dry foliage in which he hides.

Within the wholeness of primitive life, everything is alive —not just people and animals but also trees and stones and water, earth and sun and moon. Being alive, everything is necessarily particular and unique. The hunter and gatherer might not have a word for "acacia tree," but might well have a name for every particular acacia in his or her circle of existence. To cut down or hollow out a certain tree, after the proper rites, would be acceptable, but to clear out a whole area of trees according to an abstract plan would simply be unthinkable.

Along the scale of cultural evolution, abstraction and generalization tend to precede territorial or ideological war and genocide. Just as we cannot bulldoze trees in the mass until we can think of trees in the mass, so we cannot kill people in the mass until we have depersonalized them and put them into abstract categories. Whatever warfare existed prior to civilization was for honor or for bounty but rarely, if ever, for the purpose of destroying human individuals of a certain category en masse.

That masterpiece of generalization, "The only good Indian is a dead Indian," was the creation of civilized men. It went along with a brand of territorial, genocidal war that bewildered the American Indians. They finally caught on to the practice of mass warfare but were never very good at it. To the end, they never fully comprehended the grinding, joyless, deadly business of genocide.

There are various forms of mass murder, but all of them involve departicularization. The "discovery" that such entities as trees and stones are not unique beings with some sort of in-dwelling souls might have seemed a triumph of reason over superstition, but it also cleared the way for ecological rape. This same mode of thought, it has turned out, can be applied to classes of human beings: the Indians, the Japanese, the Jews, the Arabs, the blacks, the Russians. To that extent, it has served to clear the way for mass murder.

In *Little Big Man*, the Cheyenne chief, Old Lodge Skins, referring to his people as the "Human Beings," accurately sums up the difference between two modes of thought:

> "The Human Beings believe that everything is alive: not only men and animals but also water and earth and stones and also the dead things from them like this hair." But white men believe that everything is dead: stones, earth, animals, and people, even their own people. And if, in spite of that, things persist in trying to live, white men will rub them out. . . .
>
> "That," he concludes, "is the difference between white men and Human Beings."[3]

Perceptual deadness precedes mass murder. We must face the fact that abstractionists, people for whom an ideology is more important than "mere biological survival," people for whom most things already are dead, now control the secret codes that could wipe out life on this planet.

In the erotic realm, depersonalization accompanied or slightly preceded the emergence of the earliest civilized states. It was then that human beings—specifically women and slaves of both sexes—were first thought of and treated as property. We learn in the *Iliad*, for example, that the prizes for chariot-racing, boxing, wrestling, and the like included "caldrons and tripods, and horses and mules and strong oxen, and fair-girdled women, and grey iron." As for the relative value of women in that Bronze-Age culture, we learn that Achilles offered the following prizes in the wrestling match: "for the winner a great tripod for standing on the fire, prized by the Achaians among them at twelve oxen's worth; and for the loser he brought a woman into the midst, skilled in manifold work, and they prized her at four oxen."[4] The concept of women as property was clear in the polygamy that once was widely practiced in the Mohammedan countries. This was no voluptuary's storybook fantasy, but rather it was a stock-breeders' approach to marriage. It was obvious to the Arabs that one bull could service many cows and thus vastly increase wealth.

The ancient depersonalization of women had some exceptions. The Amazons might have been purely mythical—according to the legend they were forced to burn off their breasts in early childhood (*amazone*, breastless)—but the ancient Greeks considered them a very real, if short-lived, culture. And it is a matter of record that during the disturbed times around the second millennium in Egypt, the wives of pharaohs became so dominant that their husbands often ranked simply as prince-consorts.

But the Babylonian Code of Hammurabi was closer to the norm in expressing the abstracting, generalizing intellect in action, an intellect that tended to depersonalize whole classes of human beings. To take one instance, the Code allowed a husband to lodge not only his wife but also his children with a creditor as security for debts. Indeed, the theory and practice of person-as-property arose wherever there was civilization. In the third millennium B.C., prostitution was already in full swing throughout all the great oriental empires, providing a way not of owning but of leasing another human being. To say that such specialization and depersonalization is "natural" is to ignore the fact that prostitution was impossible in the way humans lived during the vast majority of their time on this planet.

Seemingly, the cruelest practice in the ancient but continuing treatment of women as property was called *suttee* in India: the requirement that the widow immolate herself on her husband's funeral pyre. Maybe it was not really the cruelest, for the widow, through will and surrender, might convince herself to go in ecstasy to the flames. No such choice is available in territorial war, where woman has always been considered (to use Nietzsche's formulation) the prize of victory, the booty of war, and the warrior's recreation.

And yet, through all of this, love and the thrill of love have somehow managed to survive. At the height of *suttee*, a marvelous breviary of love called the *Kamasutra of Vatsyana* appeared in India. As is still the practice in sex manuals, the *Kamasutra* attempted to categorize, regularize and rationalize the various acts of love. But, within these limitations, women were encouraged to take active roles and seek their own pleasure in lovemaking.

It was at the height of the Middle Ages in Europe—when the Other World seemed more real than this one and the threat of eternal damnation more vivid than any possible earthly punishment—it was precisely then that personal, passionate love reasserted itself against all the force that authority could muster. Joseph Campbell paints a memorable picture of the situation that confronted those who contemplated romance in the age of the great cathedrals:

> Marriage in the Middle Ages was an affair largely of convenience. Moreover, girls betrothed in childhood for social, economic, or political ends, were married very young, and often to much older men, who invariably took their property rights in the women they had married very seriously. They might be away for years on Crusade; the wife was to remain inviolate, and if for any reason the worm Suspicion happened to have entered to gnaw the husband's brain, his blacksmith might be summoned up to fit an iron girdle of chastity to the mortified young wife's pelvic basin. The Church sanctified these sordid property rights, furthermore, with all the weight of Hell, Heaven, eternity, and the coming of Christ in glory on the day of judgement. . . . So that, against all this, the wakening of a woman's heart to love was in the Middle Ages a grave and really terrible disaster, not only for herself, for whom torture and fire were in prospect, but also—and more horribly—in the world to come, forever. Hence, in a phrase coined by the early Church Father Tertullian, which long remained a favorite of the pulpits, woman—earthly, actual woman, that is—awakened to her nature, was *jauna diaboli*, "the devil's door."[5]

It was not primarily "sex" that threatened authority. The

aspects of life we have learned to sum up under that word could finally be dealt with through custom, taboo, and punishment. Rather, it was love—the irresistible assertion of the personal—against which authority, then and always, has mustered its most virulent opposition. An oppressive society can tolerate a great deal of sexual activity, if it can be made to run in authorized channels. The Roman Empire sanctioned orgies. Prostitution ran wild during Victoria's reign. Hitler sang the joys of procreative sex. But love—truly personal erotic love—can shake the foundations of empire and is not to be tolerated. Joseph Campbell tells us that the emergence of medieval romance—in the legends of Guinevere, and Tristan and Iseult, the story of Abelard and Heloise, the songs of the troubadours—was an event of historical significance: the birth of a new kind of myth, individual rather than collective, and a serious challenge to authority.[6]

From the beginning, civilization has required human components, something unknown and unknowable in the primitive cultures that preceded it. A component, as every engineer knows, is specialized, standardized, reliable, and predictable. In this sense, a member of a pyramid-building gang is a component, and so is a professor of comparative literature or a woman who is treated as property. Each of these specialists, at least during "working hours," is locked into a role determined by society, imprisoned in that middle realm of human existence that has been shaped by abstraction and generalization, where there is no place for either the unique or the universal.

"Sex" as we know it can exist comfortably in the component's world, but erotic love can shatter that world in an instant, in the wink of an eye. The differences between the two are conclusive.

"Sex" can be and often is specialized and standardized. Love is always unique, one of a kind.

"Sex" strives for reliability and predictability. Love is eternally surprising.

"Sex" is essentially impersonal. "Impersonal love" is a contradiction in terms.

"Sex" is a product of abstract, generalizing intellect. Love is not abstract but experiential, not general but simultaneously specific and universal. Ultimately, neither discourse nor dogma can bind it, for it is the stuff of creation itself, and thus a clear and present danger to every established order.

Borrowing the abstract idea of "sexuality" from the Victorians, the modern revolutionaries have simply turned nineteenth-century values upside down without challenging the general assumption that "sex" can be viewed and treated as apart from the rest of life. Today, the sexual specialties stand out in glaring bold-face type—straight, gay, lesbian, bisexual, transsexual—sometimes taking precedence over everything else in the lives of those involved. And there are new sexual categories: the underaged and the aging and the handicapped, the sexually inadequate male, and, of course, the sexually inadequate female. And there are subsets within subsets: "Heterosexual sex," for example, is subdivided into manual, oral, genital, and anal. Same thing for "homosexual sex." Strange to say, the power to discriminate is lost as sexual specialties are increasingly broken down and pigeonholed. We are told that no sexual category (so long as it is nonexploitative, conscious, and mutual) is to be preferred over another. Sex is sex. Getting it on is what counts. (And love is a different matter.)

How can we criticize the stated aims of the Sexual Revolution? Taken segment by segment, step by step, they make good sense. They seem benign. Only when the movement is viewed contextually, in terms of implications as well as statements, do the flaws and dangers come into focus.

For example, the idea of sex for recreation has a lilting ring to it, suggesting the beautiful young people you see on television dancing from one partner to another as a butterfly flits from flower to flower, taking pleasure and adding delight. And those who support it would be quick to point out that sex for recreation can involve caring and intimacy. But we who live in a leisure society have seen where a surfeit of recreation can take us: to frantic aimless travel, increased pollution and stress, the desecration of ancient landmarks, the trivialization of history and culture. In the same way, "recreational sex" already has led to a frantic aimless search for sensation and from there to the deadening of sensation, to sexual escalation and stress, to a desecration of courtship and romance, and to a situation in which people of both sexes often think they *should* have intercourse whether they are in love or not, whether they have anything in common, whether they even want it. And this, I suspect, has probably produced as much sexual dysfunction as it has cured, enough to keep a generation of sex therapists busy.

The modern movement toward erotic depersonalization has gone a long way in the industrial West, a long way toward Huxley's prescient *Brave New World*. But there are unmistakable signs that it will fail. Indeed, it is already failing. Sophisticated young adults, having tried the joys of sexual "freedom," are beginning to express their disillusionment—as in the *Cosmopolitan* poll cited in the Introduction and in the case of most of the people I interviewed. From the disappointments of indiscriminate sexual experimentation and open marriage springs a yearning for passionate love and commitment. "Sex" in daytime soap operas is balanced by an increase in sales of modern-day novels devoted to romance. The traditional marriage ceremony is making a comeback.

Does all this represent a movement toward Victorian mores? I don't think so. A clear majority of Americans wants nothing to do with any return to the old ways of repression and discrimination. Most people today enjoy the freedom to discuss erotic matters, to fantasize without guilt, to experiment with various modes of lovemaking, to live together without being married. But indiscriminate, obligatory "getting it on" is losing its charm. The best-kept secret of the Sexual Revolution is at last coming out of the closet. What people want most (though sometimes they can hardly bear to say it) is a return to the personal in all things, especially in erotic love.

CHAPTER NINE

Fantasy and Dogma

THE MIND is faster than the speed of light. It can spin away into space, build crystalline cities of a future that might or might not be. Just as quickly, it can fly backward in time to view dinosaurs and primal seas, and beyond that to imagine the moment of creation, when time itself was born. The mind can do another thing, in its own way even more remarkable: it can renounce the wild diversity of which it is capable and focus instead on a single image, a single sequence of events that will preoccupy it for months or years.

In erotic fantasy, we can see both these possibilities fully played out. And how strange it is that the second one so often captures us. Frustrated and fearful, we turn inward to the imagination and come upon a story that *works*. Taboos are shattered. Frustration departs. Our story is always there when we need it. What the outside world considers forbidden and shameful (we think) is comfortable and safe inside. We can use our story to excite us to orgasm or soothe us to sleep. No wonder we are reluctant to change it or let it go, this loyal companion of the night.

In Tibetan Buddhism, it is believed that intense and prolonged meditation can produce a *tulpa*, a being somewhat more than imaginary. This *tulpa*, alternately helpful and mischievous, accompanies its creator wherever he or she might go. In the same way, through our endless repetition of a single fantasy, we might find ourselves the uneasy master of an erotic *tulpa* so vivid and insistent that it intrudes upon our most intimate acts.

One woman, for instance, told me of a recurrent sex fantasy that began when she was twelve, the dreamy inhabitant of a world almost entirely dominated by horses. In her fantasy, a rough-hewn, silent cowboy would ride up in a cloud of dust, effortlessly sweep her onto his horse, and gallop away to a deserted canyon, where vague and unbelievable things would be done to her. Now in her forties, she still can summon up her cowboy in times of need. He sometimes appears, unbidden, while she is making love. Behind her closed eyelids, the cowboy is more palpable than the man who is pressing into her body at that very moment. It is not what the cowboy does to her in the canyon but rather his silent power and the breathtaking sensation of being swept up on the horse and taken away that brings her to orgasm. Give up her faithful cowboy for less reliable flights of fancy? Never.

Though fantasies are played out in the privacy of the mind, they can be strongly influenced if not shaped by the sexual climate of the culture in which they occur. We might say that a whole culture can get caught up in a single, repetitive fantasy. Psychologist Bernie Zilbergeld explores this possibility in his useful and charming book, *Male Sexuality*. According to Zilbergeld, our society's fantasy model of sex can be summed up in one phrase: "It's two feet long, hard as steel, and can go all night." He argues that the model is pervasive, appearing not only in pornography but also "in sexual humor, popular literature, those works of 'good' fiction that deal explicitly with sex, and even in technical and scientific literature."[1] He makes his point by quoting from

Harold Robbins, Mickey Spillane, Henry Miller, Norman Mailer, James Baldwin, and others, all of whom share a common preoccupation with penis size, mechanical force, male self-control, and female receptivity. One passage from Harold Robbins's *The Betsy* is sheer state of the art.

Carefully she peeled back his foreskin, exposing his red and angry glans, and took him in both hands, one behind the other as if she were grasping a baseball bat. She stared at it in wonder. *"C'est formidable. Un vrai canon. . . ."*
She almost fainted looking down at him. Slowly he began to lower her on him. Her legs came up . . . as he began to enter her. . . . It was as if a giant of white-hot steel were penetrating her vitals. She began to moan as it opened her and climbed higher into her body, past her womb, past her stomach, under her heart, up into her throat. She was panting now, like a bitch in heat. . . .
Then he was poised over her. . . . His hands reached and grasped each of her heavy breasts as if he wanted to tear them from her body. She moaned in pain and writhed, her pelvis suddenly arching and thrusting toward him. Then he entered her again.
"Mon Dieu!" she cried, the tears springing into her eyes. *"Mon Dieu!"* She began to climax almost before he was fully inside her. Then she couldn't stop them, one coming rapidly after the other as he slammed into her with the force of the giant body press she had seen working in his factory.[2]

This dream of magnitude, rigidity, and force, even as we reject it, shapes our sexual encounters more than we would care to admit, driving many of us, male and female alike, to feats of performance that have nothing to do with love or even pleasure.

In his celebrated book, *Advertisements for Myself*, Norman Mailer shows just how far the performance principle can go. One of the pieces in the book that Mailer himself tells us he particularly likes bears the title, "Time of Her Time," and concerns a certain Sergius O'Shaugnessy, who moves into a loft in Greenwich Village to set up a bullfighting school. O'Shaugnessy sees himself as "the new gun in a frontier saloon" and perceives even the most routine approach of another male as a potential threat. Sexually, he is possessed of "a kind of disinterested but developed competence":

> What it came down to was that I could go an hour with the average girl without destroying more of the vital substance than a good night's sleep could repair, and since that sort of stamina seems to be advertised, and I had my good looks, my blond hair, my height, build and bullfighting school, I suppose I became one of the Village equivalents of an Eagle Scout badge for the girls. I was one of the credits needed for a diploma in the sexual humanities ... and more than one of the girls and ladies would try me on an off-evening, like comparison-shoppers to shop the value of boyfriend, lover, mate, or husband against the certified professionalism of Sergius O'Shaugnessy.[3]

With the "noblesse oblige of the kindly cocksman," O'Shaugnessy manages to service some fifty females over the space of a year, making sure to send them away "feeling at best a little better than when they came in." His sense of largesse is tempered by a moral nicety: "I even abstained from springing too good a lay when I felt the girl was really in love with her man, and was using me only to give love the benefit of a new perspective." This saintly stud, in fact, even has the good grace to override his inevitable morning-after depression and distaste. Resisting the urge to "start the new day by lowering her in a basket out of my monk-ruined retreat six floors down to the garbage pile," he "made with the charm in the daylight and was more of a dear than most."

Then O'Shaugnessy meets his match, a stiff, spiteful Jewish girl of nineteen named Denise, a third-year student at New York University who has a passive, nice-guy Jewish boyfriend named Arthur and who is deep into psychoanalysis. On his first night with her, O'Shaugnessy discovers that Denise has never had an orgasm. He also realizes—his vast experience gives him the cue—that she is ready, that she is entering "the time of her Time." If he doesn't succeed in giving her her first orgasm, someone else will, perhaps "some bearded Negro cat who would score where I had missed and thus cuckold me in spirit." O'Shaugnessy resolves, at the risk of his manhood, to triumph over her tensions and resistances, her inane discussions of T. S. Eliot and psychoanalysis, and indeed over her specific hatred of him and her general nastiness towards the world. He will win his prize, make no mistake about it, by means of penile thrusting alone.

Drawn out over some seventeen pages, the episode resists quotation, being mostly a monotonous, exhausting recital of rage, pain, sweat, stench, nausea, hammering, drumming, pounding, jabbing, rooting, boxing, bullfighting and, as he explains, "it was like that, a hard, punishing session with pulley weights, stationary bicycle sprints, and ten breath-seared laps around the track." Finally, on the third night, his body spent to the core, his penis (he calls it "the avenger") wounded but "wild with the mania of the madman," he gives her "the first big moment of her life" by forcing his penis into her anus, then entering her vagina and cursing her.

He awakens the next morning to see Denise glaring at him with hatred rather than with the gratitude he might have expected. But never mind that.

> . . . through my hangover and the knowledge of the day and the week and the month it would take the different parts of all of me to repair, I was also knowing the taste of a reinforced will—finally, I had won. At no matter what cost, and with what luck, and with a piece of charity from her, I had won nonetheless, and since all real pay came from victory, it was more likely that I would win the next time I gambled my stake on something more appropriate for my ambition.[4]

"Time of Her Time" was written in the late fifties, and maybe it makes us uncomfortable merely because it is old enough to seem outdated yet not old enough to take on the gleam and authority of a true antique. And maybe the earlier quote from Harold Robbins should be taken merely as a piece of highly commercial writing rather than as any kind of model of our dominant fantasy. Surely by now, with so many possibilities out in the open, the old dream of force, size and performance is fading away. But maybe not.

What do the slick sex magazines tell us on this matter? Editorially, they tend to take the "enlightened" point of view: it isn't size or performance that counts, but rather feeling, responsiveness. Most of the magazines, however, publish selections of letters supposedly written by readers who are willing to bare their own sexual experiences. The letters run the gamut of sexual preference, including more oral and group sex than Norman Mailer could countenance. And there are a few gay and lesbian contributions (just about enough to match the national statistics) along with an occasional foray into bondage and sadomasochism.

Still, a familiar refrain runs through all the letters: mechanical manipulation and penetration without a hint of love and care; crude categorization and quantification of body parts. From the writing style and rhythm, the forced insertion of adjectives, the preoccupation with certain acts, the repetition of certain words and phrases, you might think that these excerpts came from a single hand rather than from various individuals pouring out their true experiences. The easiest way to explain the similarity, in fact, is to imagine one harried magazine staff member typing away in a Manhattan cubicle, glancing now and then at some reader's scrawled fantasy or boast simply to get a new setting or group of characters for one more variation on an old, well-worn theme.

We might also suspect a computer. At the present state of development, however, a computer could be programmed to come up with more novelty and surprise than is displayed here. It takes the ingenuity and doggedness of the human brain to reduce the range of erotic description to such a narrow band, to renounce the omnipotence of the imagination in the erotic realm, which involves creation itself, and opt instead for repetitive, mechanical images.

But what if, unlikely as it might seem, the letters actually were real, the unedited words of untrained writers from all over the country? That would only go to show that Zilbergeld's model persists: dogma as fantasy.

If sex is allied with creation, we might expect it to be varied and eternally surprising, especially in the fantasy realm. So long as we buy the model of size, force, and performance—*or any other dogmatic model*—we buy only limitation. The prevailing fantasy model might produce material that has a shock value suitable for aiding masturbation, but for the titillation to continue, escalation is required. Mere escalation, however, whether in fantasy or reality, assures eventual deescalation, if not repulsion and ennui. Finally, as a guide to lovemaking, this kind of material can turn out to be not only useless but quite misleading.

Mailer's Nemesis

Some years ago, while living for a short while in San Francisco's bohemian North Beach district, I happened to strike up a friendship with the neighborhood's most celebrated cocksman. His name was Charles and he was the black man that Mailer's Sergius O'Shaugnessy most feared. Charles had a scraggly beard and was shabbily dressed. Most of his front teeth were missing. Mild-mannered and unassuming, he often remained silent, listening carefully to the words of others. When he did speak, he spoke softly. Nothing about him suggested his spectacular erotic exploits. According to the stories, Charles had had intercourse with almost every white woman who made the North Beach scene. I myself had seen him with a number of beautiful women.

My friendship with Charles revolved around an old upright piano in one of the well-known beatnik bars that happened to be just around the corner from my apartment. Having no piano of my own at that time, I'd sometimes stop by after work and, more often than not, Charles would be there at the upright, drawing his own brand of desultory jazz from the chipped and uneven keys. Seeing me, he'd smile his toothless smile and make room on the bench. I'd bring a couple of beers, and we'd trade riffs and chord changes for a while and sometimes play a little three-hand jazz. He was always gentle and encouraging.

One afternoon, sitting over beers with Charles at a table in another neighborhood bar, curiosity overcame my reticence to ask him about his exploits. He had just sent away, most gently and considerately, a young blonde female with such deep, moist longing in her sky-blue eyes that my stomach ached. I turned to Charles and shook my head in wonder.

"How do you do it, Charles?"

He just smiled and kept looking at me.

"I mean, really, do you know some techniques that the rest of us don't?"

He went on smiling and shook his head.

"Or is it that you have unusual sex organs?"

He smiled even more broadly. "No, man. It's none of that."

"Well, what is it, then?"

"You really want to know, I'll tell you. What I do, you see, is cry for them. Most of them never had a man cry for them."

"You cry?"

"Yeah, I cry because they're so beautiful. I cry because it feels so *good*. Can't help myself, man. I cry all over them. They never had that."

This revelation provided me a brief moment of enlightenment, during which all of the Mailer's writings on sex (I was an admirer at the time) burst like a soap bubble. Charles's secret was out, and somebody should tell Sergius O'Shaugnessy; it might save a lot of wear and tear on his avenger. But Sergius probably wouldn't hear it. There is no place in his world for tender male tears.

Which leads us to another paradox. The ability to feel

deeply, to experience the full range of human emotions, including tears, is perhaps to possess, in Mailer's own terms, the ultimate sexual weapon. As long as the male hero deprives himself of this "weapon," he is doomed to live in fear of being cuckolded. In this perilous condition, it's no wonder that O'Shaugnessy and the countless thousands before and after him have always entered the bedroom as if it were a boxing ring. ("So my rage came back," Sergius tells us, "and we made love like two club fighters in an open exchange.") Victory or death.

The Mysteries of Woman's Sensuality

In 1940, Anaïs Nin, later to achieve celebrity as a diarist, was living in New York, the center of a small group of writers and poets. All were in dire financial straits, and the only way they could pay their bills was by writing erotica, at a dollar a page, for a book collector, who claimed he was passing the material on to an old and wealthy client. Driven by poverty, laughter and their wild poets' imagination, Nin's group turned out sexual fantasies by the ream. She chronicled their adventures in her diaries: "The homosexuals wrote as if they were women. The timid ones wrote about orgies. The frigid ones about frenzied fulfillments. The most poetic ones indulged in pure bestiality and the purest ones in perversions."

Nin organized the enterprise. She supplied paper and carbon, delivered the manuscripts anonymously, and distributed the payments. She also wrote some remarkable erotic stories. The collector paid promptly but always came back with the same request. Leave out the philosophy and analysis. Cut out the poetry. Be specific. No poetry, just sex. Nin tried to follow his instructions but found it impossible. She and her friends came to despise the man who supported them while trying to wither their imaginations. Finally, she decided to write the collector directly and tell him about their feelings.

Dear Collector: We hate you. Sex loses all its power and magic when it becomes explicit, mechanical, overdone, when it becomes a mechanistic obsession. It becomes a bore. You have taught us more than anyone I know how wrong it is not to mix it with emotion, hunger, desire, lust, whims, caprices, personal ties, deeper relationships that change its color, flavor, rhythms, intensities. . . .

The source of sexual power is curiosity, passion. You are watching its little flame die of asphyxiation. Sex does not thrive on monotony. Without feeling, inventions, moods, no surprises in bed. Sex must be mixed with tears, laughter, words, promises, scenes, jealousy, envy, all the spices of fear, foreign travel, new faces, novels, stories, dream, fantasies, music, dancing, opium, wine. . . .

There are so many minor senses, all running like tributaries into the mainstream of sex, nourishing it. Only the united beat of sex and heart together can create ecstasy.[5]

In her search for themes, Anaïs Nin read all the erotica she could lay her hands on and found it for the most part crude and shoddy. She came to the realization that for centuries we have had only one model for this literary form, that is, male sensibility, male writing. "I had a feeling," she wrote in her diary, "that Pandora's Box contained the mysteries of woman's sensuality, so different from man's and for which man's language was inadequate. The language of sex had yet to be invented. The language of the senses was yet to be explored."

This is not quite true. Nin's own erotica, first published in 1977 under the title, *Delta of Venus*, is in its own way an attempt at inventing a new erotic language. In spite of the collector's restrictions, in spite of the fact that she uses some of the customary male conventions, Nin gives us a fantasy world far different from that of Robbins or Mailer or the sex magazines.

When she looked at him she was magnetically drawn again to touch his flesh, with her mouth or hands, or with her whole body. She rubbed her whole body against his, with animal luxuriance, enjoying the friction. Then she fell on her side and lay there, touching his mouth as if she were molding it over and over again, like a blind person who wants to discover the shape of the mouth, of the eyes, of the nose, to ascertain his form, the feel of his skin, the length and texture of his hair, the shape of the hair behind his ears. Her fingers were light as she did this, then suddenly they would become frenzied, press deep into the flesh and hurt him, as if violently to assure her of his reality.

These were the external feelings of the bodies discovering each other. From so much touching they grew drugged. Their gestures were slow and dreamlike. Their hands were heavy. His mouth never closed. . . .

Because she did not quicken her movements, he changed her position, making her lie back. He crouched over her so that he could take her with more force, touching the very bottom of her womb, touching the very flesh walls again and again and then she experienced the sensation that within her womb some new cells awakened, new fingers, new mouths, that they responded to his entrance and joined in the rhythmic motion, that this suction was becoming gradually more and more pleasurable, as if the friction had aroused new layers of enjoyment. She moved quicker to bring the climax, and when he saw this, he hastened his motions inside of her and incited her to come with him, with words, with his hands caressing her, and finally with his mouth soldered to hers, so that the tongues moved in the same rhythm as the womb and penis, and the climax was spreading between her mouth and her sex, in crosscurrents of increasing pleasure, until she cried out, half sob and half laughter, from the overflow of joy through her body.[6]

Seeing irremediable flaws in the male attitude toward sex, Anaïs Nin would direct our attention, through her own writing, to feminine sensibilities, where tenderness, poetry, and all the sensual pleasures might find a home. There is truth in her analysis, but surely it is not the whole truth—

not merely male versus female, not as simple as that. Surely each mind, female or male, contains the matrix of all minds. Surely every one of us, freed from the stranglehold of cultural conditioning, could catch a glimmer of every erotic proclivity, every nuance, every strange and errant desire. And surely there must be a way, through deep surrender to fantasy and surprise, to visit the creative opening in the circle of existence, the source of endless novelty and invention.

The Dogma of the Enlightened

It would seem reasonable to suppose that the mind, unencumbered by gravity and momentum, would enjoy a freedom impossible in actual experience. But the mind is the instrument not only of imagination but of dogma as well. Our power to abstract, to build mental structures, is also our disability. An idea can become so compelling that we mistake it for reality, mistake the map for the territory. Idea becomes ideology becomes dogma, creation's deadliest adversary.

There is something particularly insidious, in fact, in what might be termed the dogma of the enlightened. Take the matter of penis size. Among the sexually enlightened, as we have seen, the size of the male organ is said to have nothing to do with female pleasure. It is, we are told, a matter of no consequence whatever. And who would want to question a doctrine that would do so much to relieve male anxiety and remedy feelings of male inadequacy?

The trouble is that even this humane dogma isn't invariably true, especially in the realm of fantasy. Down through the ages, the fully erect, sometimes outsize penis has been seen as an embodiment of creative energy, of the vital force itself. This is vividly depicted in Paleolithic cave paintings showing shamans with elongated, shaftlike phalluses and in the giant *lingam* sculpture of the third and second millennia B.C. throughout the Indus valley, in the extravagant penises of feudal Japan's *shunga* or sexual picture books, and in the phallus-headed birds that appear so frequently in later European art as well as in Paleolithic times—clear representations of the male organ as a winged thought.

And it would seem that neither mere accident nor biological necessity could account for the fact that human genitalia are especially large among primates. Darwinian selection in this matter must be at least to some extent erotic and aesthetic. The appeal of the well-formed male organ survives in the pornography of all cultures. Only the most absolute ascetic could view the phallic capacity to expand and penetrate and inseminate as less than magnificent: a powerful, primal idea captured in flesh and blood, gravity and time. And in the female genitalia as well, for the clitoris and the underlying flesh of the labia as well as of the penis are made of the same kind of erectile tissue. Female creative force is symbolized in the expanded flesh of breast and pelvis so familiar in cave paintings; *lingam* power in Indian art is matched by *yoni* power. All this suggests that both female and male are equally capable of expressing erotic feelings through physical transformation.

The current male fantasy model ("It's two feet long, hard as steel, and can go all night") is misleading and ultimately disabling. But so is any dogma to the contrary, for the very essence of the erotic is its unpredictability. Perhaps the dream of size, rigidity, and force will maintain its power over us only so long as we keep denying the primal symbolism from which it is descended. The problem with Robbins, Mailer, and the sex magazines is not the crude hyperbole, but the mechanical, essentially abstract quality of the interactions, the lifelessness, the ultimately unerotic effect. There is another approach. Give Robbins his due, and forget him. Award Sergius O'Shaugnessy a Purple Heart for his wounded avenger and let it go at that. Why not, rather than constructing an opposing dogma, move into an entirely new area, toward the infinite variety and surprise of creation?

At the most fundamental level, it is fear that prevents

motion. Horrified by Victorian proscription, we seek safety in contrary prescription. Threatened by unrealistic standards of size and performance, we find sanctuary in an opposing dogma, also limiting. Our timidity is not unjustified. Outside the sanctuary, beyond dogma, the winds of the imagination are strong and unpredictable. Shocking erotic images appear from nowhere. Atavistic lusts seem to threaten the stability of our relationships. No wonder we are tempted to retreat into dogma. One of the main appeals of both pornography and anti-pornography is a common predictability: both are essentially safe.

To experience the erotic pure and clear, without hypothesis, is often to approach the edge of terror. "I have very powerful orgasms," one woman told me, "and I'm aware of holding back because I'm afraid of what would happen if I really let go. I'm afraid of the intensity of my love, of getting hurt if I surrendered completely. But that's only a part of my reluctance. You see, I sometimes get very close to going even further into my orgasms, and that's when I sense the enormousness of it, so I hold back. But one night not long ago, something happened—I had known it was coming and yet it was a surprise—and I totally surrendered. It was beyond anything I'd ever experienced. It was like being catapulted out into space. The word 'thrill' would be a pale description. In a strange way, it was what you go to horror movies for—to be shocked out of your seat. More than that, it was a mystery revealed, a magnificently powerful experience. And I must say it verified my fear, because I realized I could go even further—and that was *really* terrifying."

At the moment of orgasm, all fantasies are obliterated, and the most powerful episodes of lovemaking are perhaps fantasyless. Still, fantasies can help guide us toward those moments in which they themselves disappear. It might be said, in fact, that fantasies make up the interior erotic culture and, thus, that to enrich our fantasy life is to enhance the entire erotic life. I, for one, would like to take every fantasy that enters my mind simply as a gift from the universe, without expectation or judgement. And I would not want to withhold anything in my mind from the mind of my lover.

Dogma freezes the erotic play, prevents its further evolution. Fantasy, on the other hand, allows us to tap into the wellspring of creativity and test the stuff of existence in relative safety. To be creative in love, or anything else, requires that we distinguish between fantasy and dogma. To remain sane requires that we distinguish between fantasy and reality.

CHAPTER TEN

The Person and the Pigeon

OUR EROTIC experience is deeply influenced by our view of the person, our feelings about human nature. If in our heart of hearts we look upon the human individual as essentially a monster or an object, our intimate relationships are severely limited and deformed, no matter how much we know about "sex." But to see the human individual as potentially loveable and unique in all the universe permits us to surrender to the nearly limitless possibilities of love.

The darker view often prevails. One of the most pessimistic thinkers on this matter was the seventeenth-century philosopher, Thomas Hobbes, who saw every human being as driven by "a perpetual and restlesse desire of Power after power, that ceaseth only in Death."[1] Power, for Hobbes, meant power over others, and he believed that if social restraints were removed, each of us would be continually subject to violent invasion of our life and property. Hobbes maintained that our only hope lay in voluntarily handing over all our rights and powers to a sovereign of some sort, who would maintain order. Otherwise, we would stand in danger of quickly reverting to our "natural" state, in which life is "solitary, poore, nasty, brutish and short."[2]

Views similar to Hobbes's are commonplace in Western thought, nowhere with more force and drama than in the later works of Sigmund Freud:

> The element of truth behind all this, which people are so ready to disavow, is that men are not gentle creatures who want to be loved, and who at the most can defend themselves if they are attacked; they are, on the contrary, creatures among whose instinctual endowments is to be reckoned a powerful share of aggressiveness. As a result, their neighbour is for them not only a potential helper or sexual object, but also someone who tempts them to satisfy their aggressiveness on him, to exploit his capacity for work without compensation, to use him sexually without his consent, to seize his possessions, to humiliate him, to cause him pain, to torture and to kill him.[3]

If this evaluation is correct, a prudent man or woman would rarely, if ever, be willing to enter that state of vulnerability that is prerequisite to erotic love at its best and highest. What woman in her right mind would open her body and soul to the monster Freud describes, would willingly let him inside the delicate passageway to her womb? And no wonder so many men shudder at the old myth of *vagina dentata*, the vagina within which hidden teeth are embedded.

Those who assume that beneath the veneer of civilization there lurks a vicious human beast must approach the erotic warily, as a matter of combat and subterfuge. For the man, there is pursuit, strategy, conquest. For the woman, enticement, wiles, submission—then, at last, the monster shamed and tamed. This situation sometimes turns upside down; the woman becomes a multi-orgasmic pursuer and the man a bewildered victim. But as long as we think of the person as basically monstrous, nothing has really changed. "Sex" is possible. Some sort of war between the sexes is probable. Erotic surrender is unlikely.

Pessimistic views of the person, of human nature, are particularly popular in this century of outrages. But there is another way of explaining the outrages. Perhaps the conditions imposed by civilized society create the very viciousness that society is then called upon to repress. Notable among those who have held this view is the eighteenth-century philosopher Jean-Jacques Rousseau, a key figure in the French Enlightenment and an influence on the American Revolution. Rousseau's contemporary, the encyclopedist Denis Diderot, commented: "The philosophy of M. Rousseau of Geneva is almost the inverse of that of Hobbes. The one believes man by nature good, the other believes him evil. According to the philosopher of Geneva, the state of nature is a state of peace; according to the philosopher from Malmesbury, it is a state of war. . . . Both of them exaggerate."[4]

Any absolute statement about human nature is obviously an exaggeration. Still, anthropological studies unavailable to Freud and those who preceded him favor Rousseau's exaggeration over Hobbes's. Freud went on the assumption that primitive societies were more warlike than civilized societies. The great majority of modern anthropologists hold that the opposite is true, that the more "advanced" a society is, the more likely it is to be warlike. In his monumental study of warfare among 653 primitive societies, Quincy Wright concludes: "The collectors, lower hunters and lower agriculturalists are the least warlike. The higher hunters and higher agriculturalists are more warlike, while the highest agriculturalists and the pastors are the most warlike of all."[5] Our primitive ancestors did not live in Eden, but in all probability, their life involved less greed, less fighting, and less aggression in general than does life in civilization. Too long have we slandered our forebears! The familiar cartoon showing a caveman holding a club and dragging a woman by her hair has nothing to do with the Stone Age. Could it be our secret, shameful vision of our modern world?

But my purpose here is not to argue innate human goodness or badness. Rather, I wish to propose that a shift in our perceptions on this matter can cause a shift in our erotic experience. To mention an example, in *The Anatomy of Human Destructiveness* Erich Fromm concludes from wide research and penetrating thought that the human individual is by no means naturally or instinctually evil or untrustworthy. If words can change perception, reading Fromm's book could possibly be of more benefit to one who is having trouble with erotic trust and surrender than could any sex manual.[6]

It might well be, in fact, that trust, in philosopher Sam Keen's memorable phrase, is the most powerful aphrodisiac. Trust requires at the least a modicum of faith in the human potential for love, honesty, and loyalty, a faith that begins with and is reflected in trust in one's self. In these sex-sated days, we can easily forget the awesome surrender involved in a non-manipulative, unconditional act of love. A leap into trust is involved in every such joining. The process is circular: just as trust is necessary for transcendent erotic experience so that experience can create deeper trust in human possibilities.

The Person as Object

To perceive the individual as essentially monstrous is clearly a hindrance to erotic surrender. To perceive the individual as an object can lead to even worse difficulties, for that perception is both more subtle and more pervasive, thus harder to root out.

In Chapter Eight, I outlined the profound shift in perception that accompanied the transformation from primitive to civilized existence: the long, slow dying of the visible and invisible world. We saw that once everything was alive—every stone, every tree, every stream—and that all the world was perceived and experienced as personal. Then came abstraction, generalization, and classification: powerful tools for social organization and the control of nature. Stone, tree, and stream were depersonalized and separated from nature's web, as things to be used. Existence became more manipulative than relational. Even human individuals—this idea would be terribly shocking were we not so accustomed to it—began to be seen and treated as things, as means for achieving various purposes, in the fields and marketplace, at work and at war. Nor were erotic relationships immune from the great epidemic of depersonalization that swept across the earth with the dying of hunting and gathering. Women and sometimes men became sexual property, breeding stock, pawns in the power game of alliances.

Today, we celebrate our freedom from traditional sexual constraints by devising ingenious new modes of depersonalization. We see the person as object whenever we use the erotic for some essentially selfish purpose: to gain status, to realize a fantasy, to "enhance self-image," to "have a healthy sex life." We see the person as object in the persistent categorization and quantification of sex studies, in the popular obsession with sexual typology, physical measurements, and frequency and duration of intercourse. A recent movie entitled *10* is based on the current practice of rating sex partners on a scale of one to ten according to external appearance. Is there any way to perceive a "10" other than as an object?

Buber and Skinner

Martin Buber's *I and Thou* first appeared in Germany under the title *Ich und Du* in 1923. Since then, it has been translated into most of the world's major languages and has become an essential document in the literature of the personal versus the impersonal. According to Buber, we live in a twofold world, depending upon whether in our hearts we say "I-It" or "I-Thou." When we see a person "objectively," as a thing to be observed and acted upon, we are in an I-It world: the I is perfectly alone, and the external world is relevant only to the extent that it enters the I. But when we involve ourselves with a person in a mutual relationship, holding back nothing, we are in an I-Thou world. The whole universe is seen in light of the Thou and not the Thou in the light of the universe; calculation and manipulation are impossible.

An I-It relationship is caught in the chain of cause and effect and actually exists only in the past, for all objective knowledge about a person is about what *has been* rather than what *is*. But an I-Thou relationship escapes the causal chain entirely, existing only in the eternal present and involving the total unpredictability of human freedom. It is here, in the moment, that creation is possible. The world of I-It may be seen as safe and practical, and all of us must deal with it in our everyday lives. Ultimately, however, it is empty. Buber tells us that "without *It* man cannot live. But he who lives with *It* alone is not a man."[7]

Buber's distinctions become clear in the religious context, for God is the one *Thou* that can never become an *It*. We can also say that erotic relationships ideally must take place in an I-Thou world. The unhappy truth is that they generally do not. There may be those fine, fair moments of total surrender when the whole universe is seen in the light of the beloved. But then *It* creeps in. The beloved becomes an object. "Sex" becomes an item, a reinforcement. And, sooner than we might think possible, we find ourselves in a Skinnerian world.

Working for Shocks

For those who admire science at its most rigorous and elegant, the theories of Professor B. F. Skinner, of Harvard, hold particular appeal. It is almost as if the formulations of Sir Isaac Newton on the motion of physical objects could be applied to the behavior of living organisms. According to Skinner's theory, behavior is more effectively shaped by reward—he calls it positive reinforcement—than by punishment. This much might seem fairly obvious, but Skinner goes further. What is used as reward is not nearly so important in shaping behavior as is the particular schedule on which the reward is offered.

Take a hungry pigeon in a cage fitted with a device that can be set to reward it with grains of corn for the act of pecking a key. First, the pigeon is rewarded or "reinforced" on a regular schedule, say one grain of corn after every five pecks. The rate and pattern of pecking is automatically recorded. Next, the pigeon is reinforced on a variable schedule. The grains of corn are doled out randomly—a grain after every eight pecks, a grain after every two pecks and so on—but still at an average rate of one grain for every five pecks. On this *variable ratio*, the pigeon pecks faster and more regularly.

What we have learned so far is that a variable ratio of reinforcement gets more work out of the pigeon than does a regular ratio. But there is still another schedule of reinforcement, one that has terrible implications for human behavior and helps explain the power struggle that so often develops in long-term intimate relationships. Let us call it the *variable stretching ratio* of reinforcement.

Take the same hungry pigeon, working fairly hard and regularly for an average of one grain of corn for every five pecks, doled out on a variable schedule. Still using the variable ratio, stretch out the average interval between reinforcements—one grain for every ten pecks on an average, then one for every twenty-five pecks, then fifty pecks, one hundred pecks, and so on. What happens? The pigeon works harder and harder. The pecks become almost continuous. What's more, after the final grain of corn is doled out, the pigeon goes on pecking far longer than with any other schedule. In fact, if the schedule has been stretched out ingeniously enough, the pigeon will peck *tens of thousands* of times before giving up.

Though it might be hard to imagine, a pigeon can also be

taught to work for a painful shock. As in the previous case, the pigeon learns to peck a key for grains of corn. Then shocks of gradually increasing intensity are given *along with* the corn. Finally, the corn is gradually withdrawn, leaving only the shocks. The pigeon goes on working for the "reward" of being shocked.

To prove that the schedule of reinforcement rather than the particular reinforcement is what most determines behavior, Skinnerians can show you a pigeon on a variable stretching ratio of reinforcement working frantically to get shocked, then going on pecking tens of thousands of times after the last shock has been administered in the vain hope (it's only fair to say that a Skinnerian would never use the word "hope" in this situation) of just one more shock.

Professor Skinner has tried hard, through studies, essays, and books, to prove that his laws of reinforcement apply to human beings as well as to organisms such as rats and pigeons. It is sobering to note how often he seems to be right.

One Couple's Story

Let us look at the erotic history of a young couple we'll call Bob and Joan. The names and some details have been changed but this story, which demonstrates the power of reinforcement schedules, is true. At the beginning of their marriage, Bob and Joan were the envy and delight of all who knew them. They were good looking, well-to-do, flushed with the fresh, untroubled sensuality of youth. For both Bob and Joan, making love was like rejoining some lost part of themselves. Nothing was planned. There were no negotiations. They were children at play. Each was *Thou* for the other.

After a few months, the initial storm of their passion subsided, and their lovemaking settled into a more moderate schedule. It was only at this point that a slight disparity emerged: though the two of them seemed equally in love, though each truly desired the other, Bob's erotic appetite turned out to be slightly greater than Joan's. Neither mentioned this to the other. At the beginning, in fact, both repressed all conscious knowledge of the disparity.

But there was a subtle change in their relationship. With no clear awareness of what was happening, they slipped into new roles. Bob became the petitioner and Joan the granter of favors. Joan took the part of the reinforcer and Bob became the reinforced.

For a while, the change brought no problems. The couple's love life might have seemed even more interesting than before. Bob found himself doing certain favors, performing certain extra services for his wife—because he loved her so much, he supposed. And the lovemaking that sometimes followed his thoughtfulness was particularly appreciated. He also found himself devising ever more ingenious ways of arousing his wife. This, too, added something to the erotic relationship in the way of innovation and spiciness. The only trouble was that Bob, involved in his calculations, was not really present; during the act of love, he was sometimes still thinking up strategies.

Joan was also caught up in this Skinnerian web. Reinforcement works both ways. (Skinner himself has pointed out that his pigeons have changed him more than he has changed them.) Without knowing what was happening, Joan was rewarded and shaped by her behavior, that is, withholding sex on a random basis. For a while, in any case, the many rewards she received gave her no reason for dissatisfaction.

But the crux of the matter was that both lovers were unwittingly becoming objects for each other, and the act of love was becoming a commodity, an item of reinforcement.

Then Joan got pregnant. After a short bout with morning sickness, she and her husband regained the careless sensuality of their first weeks together. For Joan, it was perhaps the infusion of hormones that increased her desire. But, more likely, it was simply the change of context, the joint creation of a new life, that jarred them out of the web in which they had been trapped, gave them passage once again to world of spontaneity and mutuality that Buber captures in the term, I-Thou. In any case, the two of them enjoyed the sweetness of erotic love without calculation or manipulation up to the last two or three weeks of her pregnancy.

Ronnie's birth was normal, and he was an easy baby; he slept past dawn on his first night home. There was money enough for a full-time maid for the first three months. Bob and Joan had mutual interests, a nice house and good friends. By all rights, their rich, happy life should have continued.

Indeed, the two of them could hardly wait for the day Joan's doctor had set for a resumption of sexual relations. And there was a brief period when love was sunny again. Within a few weeks, though, Joan's libido began diminishing. What was going on? Maybe it was just that Joan was turning a large portion of her love toward Ronnie, leaving less for her husband. And there was a possible psychoanalytical interpretation: Joan had always been extremely close to her father. Now Bob was cast in a father role. Perhaps she was subconsciously resisting a symbolically incestuous relationship.

But this sort of analysis pales beside the raw fact that both Bob and Joan were falling into a variable stretching ratio of reinforcement. The instances of intercourse went from two or three times a week to once a week to once every two weeks or less, on what seemed a purely random schedule. Bob began to think that what he did or said had little or nothing to do with Joan's arousal; it was if he was not even part of the equation. His hurt turned to resentment turned to anger. For Joan's part, she was increasingly turned off by her husband's erotic calculation, the constant pressure she felt from him, the mechanical, seemingly unfeeling quality of his arousal. At the same time, she was feeling more and more guilty for being cold, for rebuffing Bob's advances. Her guilt turned to resentment and then to anger.

Often, even worse, hurt and guilt went underground, manifesting itself not in open anger but in what is commonly thought of as a power struggle: recriminations for past actions, words and deeds of petty sabotage, endless debates on such matters as household responsibilities, social behavior, the right to make decisions.

At the same time, Bob and Joan finally acknowledged that they "had a sex problem." They tried to talk out the problem. The talk was oblique and blaming. Joan wanted them to go into therapy. Bob refused. Like many men, he feared giving up control. He wanted to handle things himself. Instead of therapy, he started a surreptitious love affair with a woman at his office.

In his own mind, Bob had to force himself to take the first step in the affair. Once it was taken, however, he found himself deeply, passionately involved. Lovemaking was fantastic. Even better, his manhood was validated. The woman fell head over heels in love with him and he fancied he was in love with her. The affair escalated. The two of them became careless, blatant. Bob was vaguely uncomfortable. Was he using her? Was she only a pawn in his struggle with his wife?

Matters came to a head. The woman wanted him to get a divorce, and he realized he didn't want to. Joan began voicing her suspicions. (Perhaps at some level she had known all along.) There were stormy scenes of accusation and denial. Finally Bob confessed everything, renounced his affair, asked Joan to take him back.

There was a moment of confusion, then a miracle. Husband and wife looked into each other's eyes as if for the first time. Tears streamed down their faces. All manipulation and control fell away. They met in the moment, totally vulnerable and open. For two days, without calculation or reserve, they alternately wept and made love. Love and passion flowed in a single, crystal-clear stream. They assumed their troubles were over. A love so well-tested as theirs would never fail again.

But they asked too much of the miracle. When passion lost

some of its momentum, they tried to force it. Again Bob became manipulative. Again Joan withdrew. Again sex became a commodity and the mates became objects for each other. The variable stretching ration of reinforcement reasserted itself. The power struggle that accompanied it resumed.

And now there was another factor to be reckoned with. The couple had received a valuable reward for Bob's having had an affair then returning to his wife. According to Skinner's formulation, this reinforcement increased the probability of Bob's having another affair. Less than two years later, that's just what happened. There was another reconciliation, but this time the miracle was a little frayed around the edges. Then, tit for tat, it was Joan's turn to have an affair. Hers ended somewhat differently, but actually everything was becoming more and more the same.

A second pregnancy changed the context of the relationship less than had the first one, but kept the couple together long enough to submit themselves to marriage counseling. Two years of counseling taught them how to communicate more clearly and with less blaming. Better communication revealed that their conflict now extended to almost every area of their lives and that they would perhaps do just as well to split. But by now they had their two children, their new suburban house, and their history. Strangely, too, they seemed perversely drawn to their ordeal.

Near the end, Bob and Joan became addicted to the pain they were causing each other and themselves. Like Skinner's pigeon, they were working for shocks. On the rare occasions they "had sex"—it was just that—they were both sorry afterwards. Their arguments subsided, yet people felt uncomfortable around them. They knew they should separate but were held together for years longer by what seemed to them an inexplicable force. Finally, nothing was left except a skeleton of a marriage. Yet when the couple did divorce, both experienced severe stress: depression, anxiety, inexplicable illness.

The marriage I have just descibed has its own particulars,

but is by no means atypical. After years of study, marriage experts William J. Lederer and Don D. Jackson found that a "stable-satisfactory" marriage is "almost hypothetical." "We have never observed," they write, "a generally constant collaborative union between spouses during the period when they are raising children."[8] But expert testimony is hardly needed in a society where the number of loving, stable, creative long-term erotic relationships in any circle of friends is likely to be low indeed.

Entering a Different World

What can be done? Therapies abound these days. The bookshelves are heavy with sexual solutions. The books proposing open marriage, much in evidence a decade or so ago, have for the most part made their way to the bargain tables. The best of the current sex books have arrived at a sort of consensus. Each partner should be able to speak openly and freely, making needs known without demanding or even expecting that they be fulfilled by the other. Genital penetration followed by orgasm is not the sole purpose of lovemaking. Better to approach the erotic encounter as a process involving gentle touch and talk and having no specific goal. Orgasm can be reached by means other than penetration, and thus the less aroused partner can be relieved of performance pressure.

All good advice. It is also helpful to know that schedules of reinforcement exist, that human beings as well as pigeons can get unconsciously hooked on patterns of behavior that are not to their own best interests. Skinner's formulations are finally reductive, but he remains an excellent guide on how *not* to live. Once aware of the possibility of being controlled by a destructive reinforcement schedule, a human being (who, after all, is not a pigeon) can devise ways to break the schedule.

But what I have in mind goes beyond control and countercontrol, beyond calculation and manipulation. It involves entering a different world, a world in which sexual intercourse is not thought of or treated as an item or a commodity, but rather as a spontaneous, unconditional expression of love. It is a world in which your erotic partner is thought of or treated not as an object but as a *person*, a sacred being encompassing the universe. It is a world of great personal risk, for in it calculation is impossible, everything is offered up, and no place is left to hide. It is a world, in short, of I and Thou, a splendid place in spite of the risks, where the chains of the past are broken, power struggles are reduced in importance, and schedules of reinforcement are simply irrelevant.

It might be unrealistic to suggest that we should live in the realm of I-Thou all of the time or even most of the time. But the act of love is intimate and powerful and, no matter how we try to reduce it, allied with creation itself. Surely (love being what it is) there are moments when we can approach our lover as *Thou*, moments without judgement or expectation. Each such moment becomes a redemption from time and calculation, a journey to the place of creation where new information enters the universe and new beginnings are always possible. To sojourn in the I-Thou world is to renew the weariest love and reawaken the primal erotic joy that no book of sexual "positions" can ever produce. It is also true that in this world (and if this is only a side effect, it is a blessed one) the familiar sexual "problems" lose their power over our lives and indeed are often "cured."

To perceive the human individual as a monster or as an object is obviously to lose all hope of entering the world of I and Thou. A different, positive way of viewing the individual is introduced in Chapter Twelve.

CHAPTER ELEVEN

A Body Well-Suited for War

THE BODY has long been viewed as an object, an instrument, and an ornament. At most times and in most places since the Pyramid Age, it has been thought of as separate from if not opposed to the spirit and the intellect. Utilized as a sort of machine of gratification and procreation, the body has contributed to the abstraction and fragmentation of erotic experience. Only now are we beginning to realize the body's influence on every aspect of our lives, not only on how we make love, digest food, work, and play, but also on how we think and how we feel about others.

In prehistoric times, as far as we can tell from anthropology, the body and world were essentially indivisible. And there was a graceful interlude in ancient Greece—we still see it in the masterpieces of classical sculpture—when the unity of body, mind, and spirit was simply assumed. But that time of grace was short-lived. Even while the poet Pindar was singing the glories of embodiment, the ancient games at Olympia, Pytho, Nemea, and the Corinthian Isthmus were falling prey to professionalism, bribery, and cheating. By the time of Alexander the Great, Olympic athletes were generally held in disrepute. Even earlier, in the thought of Plato and others, the entire physical realm had come to be considered a mere shadow of a realm of ideal forms, with physical love a poor imitation of spiritual love.

Ever since the Greeks, in fact, the great majority of our religious leaders and philosophers either have ignored or denigrated the body. Thomas a Kempis referred to it as "this dung heap." St. Francis wavered between chastising it and reluctantly cooperating with what he called "Brother Body" or "Brother Ass." Today, the *Encyclopedia of Philosophy* has nothing at all under "body." There is only a bare heading, "Body-Mind Problem," directing the reader to an article that puts things in their proper order: "Mind-Body Problem."

We remember the English and American Victorians for their intense fascination with and aversion toward the erotic. But their notions about the body itself were perhaps even more bizarre. Here in the United States, the attacks on carnality were led by Sylvester Graham, a lay preacher who invented the Graham cracker and inspired the invention of cold breakfast cereal. Graham started out early in the nineteenth century as a temperance lecturer. In the 1830s, however, he and a small army of like-minded "experts" turned their attention to the evils of sexuality—not only that, in fact, but to the evils of all bodily feelings.

Graham saw the body as a fortress under seige and the senses as sentinels against the approach of dangers from an inevitably hostile outside world. The distinction between inside and outside, he warned, must be cleared and absolute. Dreams and fantasies were seen as mild forms of insanity. Even the mental images that arise from memory or imagination could be dangerous, since they might distract the attention from the outside environment.

In this context, sexual desire was seen as a sickness and the sex act itself a catastrophe. Graham warned that only when a man reaches thirty is his body mature enough to withstand the trauma of copulation. Even then, he should restrict this activity to a bare minimum: once a month for the healthy and robust, less or none at all for the sickly and sedentary. The consequences of too much sex (more than once a month) are truly terrible. Graham's inventory of afflictions, just those caused by libidinal excess between wife and husband, ran to thirty-nine diseases, from impaired vision and pulmonary consumption to genital disorder and loss of memory. These views might now seem laughable, but in the 1830s they were taken quite seriously. Graham's teaching, as a matter of fact, became a major influence in American sex-hygiene manuals that were in some cases still being used at the time of World War II.

After Graham's death in 1851, the attacks on the body only increased in intensity. The effect, significantly, was to make the whole body ever more shameful, to turn the individual's attention and energy, not to the spirit, but almost entirely to the outside world.

The sexual fallacies promulgated by Graham and other Victorians have generally been exposed for what they are, and Victorian erotic attitudes and values, if not truly transformed, have obviously been turned upside down. Our view of the body, however, has proven far more resistant to change. Today, it is possible to be sexually liberated and still to make many assumptions about the body that would be quite agreeable to Sylvester Graham. The Victorian view, shaped by nineteenth-century mechanism as well as prudery, is only an extreme version of a persisting myth, which might be summarized as follows:

The body is separate from and often opposed to mind and spirit.

The body is also separate from and often opposed to the surrounding environment. It is essentially a *container* for life, consciousness, self.

The self, generally considered to reside in the head, commands the body to do its will, as a master commands a servant.

The body often resists the will of its master, and must be disciplined to perform as a useful and ethical instrument of the self.

Messages from the body, except as signals of sickness or injury, are to be distrusted. Far from being an aid, the body is a hindrance to cognitive learning and moral action.

What emerges from these assumptions is a body well suited to war, conquest, and the exploitation of nature—enterprises that require large numbers of people who can ignore the feelings of others and any feeling for the balance of nature. To ignore the feelings of others, it is best to be cut off from your own feelings. To ignore the needs of nature, it is best to be out of touch with your own natural bodily needs.

How can a society produce unfeeling, out-of-touch people? Through early toilet training, taboos on touch and all sensual pleasures, physical punishment, rigid educational practices; by muting emotional expression in men while demeaning it in women and confining erotic activity as much as possible to procreation. Such practices lead to the view of the body outlined above. That view of the body also leads to such practices. Which came first—vision or practice—is hard to say, for the two are mutually linked.

But vision is pervasive and persistent. Most psychotherapists, for example, now decry early toilet training, yet a majority of them still defer to the imperial mind, insisting that therapy be limited to talk alone, with absolutely no use of bodily movement, breathing exercises, or touch. And the slick magazines, while eagerly promoting sexual expressiveness and experimentation, keep right on presenting a body that is more than ever an object—photographed and airbrushed to stand out from the background in high definition, classified by age, weight, and measurements like a side of meat.

The foundations of our conventional view of the body go back a long way in Western history. The extreme Victorian version, however, emerged during a period of unprecedented conquest and exploitation. Between 1830 and the beginning of World War I, Europeans swarmed over the globe in ever-increasing numbers to create colonies and control lives. In America, the white people of the eastern third of the nation swept westward to swallow a continent whole, condemning the former inhabitants to death or life on reservations. During the same period, the Industrial Revolution made its first real impact on Europe and America, not only advancing imperialism but also promoting the rape of nature: forests leveled, hills gouged, rectangular grids laid over the sinuous curves of the earth.

A warlike, exploitative society created a body to match, and that body created a warlike, exploitative society, which finally tried to destroy itself in the cataclysms of two world wars. This relationship between body and body politic is noted in the theories of neurophysiologist James W. Prescott, of the U.S. National Institutes of Health. Using anthropological, psychological, and neurological data, Prescott argues persuasively that deprivation of body pleasure, especially during infancy, childhood, and adolescence, is very closely tied to the amount of warfare and violence in any given society. He also blames other maladies on what he terms "somatosensory deprivation":

> Derived from the Greek word for "body," the term refers to the sensations of touch and body movement which differ from the senses of sight, hearing, smell, and taste. I believe that the deprivation of body touch, contact and movement are the basic causes of a number of emotional disturbances which include depressive and autistic behaviors, hyperactivity, sexual aberration, drug abuse, violence, and aggression.[1]

Years earlier, Wilhelm Reich pointed out that the ideology

of a given society anchors itself in a particular character structure and that the institutions of the society serve to produce that very character structure. Reich maintained, moreover, that character structure is reflected in the structure of the body. Character armor against the expression of emotion is manifested in constricted, permanently spasmed muscle tissue. According to Reich, character armor and muscular armor are functionally identical.[2]

Since Reich's death in 1957, Reichians, neo-Reichians, and "body workers" of a bewildering variety and profusion have struggled to free the body from its muscular armoring. They have had some success. (The torturous marriage between body and society is difficult to dissolve.) But even a brief experience of a relaxed, supple, expressive body gives a glimpse of a different way of living, a changed society. A shift in the way we experience our bodies—produced not only through "body work" and a new body awareness but also through the fitness boom—is indeed an important part of what a number of social researchers see as a sweeping, irreversible cultural revolution in America. Opinion polls show that during the 1970s ever-increasing numbers of Americans shifted their priorities from narrow economic self-interest and the conquest of nature to the realization of creative, nonmaterialistic quality of experience.[3]

But polls are not needed to show that the times call for new values, a new character structure, a new view of the body. The physical frontier is gone, and with it the need for a warlike Victorian body. The instruments of nuclear holocaust are in place. The self-destruction that was attempted in World War I and World War II is now possible; the means of destroying the biosphere are at hand. Further conquest, exploitation, and mass warfare are now counterproductive on even the most selfish and rapacious terms. It is becoming more and more apparent that the world has become too small and too dangerous for the outmoded yet persistent Victorian body.

In any case, it is a body ill-suited for love (nor is it a good body for athletic excellence). Armored muscles and a constricted pelvis misshape the passions; twisted perceptions limit love. Trapped in a container of obdurate flesh and condemned to fight off attacks from a hostile outer environment while stifling immoral, untrustworthy inner urges, even a consummate romantic is in no condition for surrender and commitment. "Sex" might work. Pursuit, titillation, romantic melodrama, and momentary spasm might relieve the pain and unease of living in the armored body; but it doesn't take long for pain and unease to reassert themselves. Then it's pursuit, titillation, melodrama, and spasm again.

The magical moments of love and creation sometimes pop up out of nowhere, even during the frantic pursuit of recreative sex: tantalizing intimations that discontent may have an end. But the Victorian body—rigid, armored, and *out of touch*—is allergic to lasting love and will find a way to cast it out. Then again and yet again, it's on to another amorous conquest, another needless purchase, another pointless trip, another war.

Society, erotic love, and the body are inextricably connected. To change one is ultimately to change the others. The process of change is complex and intricate, mediated through countless feedback loops. Our vision of the body figures in this process. It is a key, an entry point to transformation. How might we revision the body? One possibility is treated in chapter 13. All of the next section, in fact, is devoted to positive ways of perceiving erotic experience.

PART IV

Revisioning the Erotic

CHAPTER TWELVE

Radical Repersonalization

A POSITIVE VIEW of the erotic requires a positive view of the person, of human possibilities. Such a view might well begin with two qualities that I see as absolutely irreducible in every human individual: *personal identity* and *holonomy*. Through personal identity, each of us expresses the multiplicity of the universe. Through holonomy, each of us expresses the oneness of all existence. Thus, each human being might be thought of as both unique and universal, which is to say, far more than a monster or an object.

To understand *personal identity*, we start with one of life's most profound mysteries—that no two faces are alike. The ineluctable uniqueness of each human individual also expresses itself in fingerprint, voiceprint, signature, scent, breathing pattern, brainwave, and indeed in every way of moving, every aspect of being. Uniqueness is encoded in the genes with their elongated, intertwining molecules of DNA, which are found in every cell in the body, with the exception of the red blood cells. (If red corpuscles contained DNA, blood transfusions would be impossible, since the body would reject the donor's blood as foreign matter.)

The DNA molecule, at essence, is not really a "thing" but rather a formal, rhythmic dance.

In fact, when we get down to the elementary particles of which all matter is made, we discover not static substance but patterns and rates of vibration—in Einstein's words, "pulselike concentrations of fields that stick stably together." When these vibrant fields, these waves in space-time, are joined in a coherent, self-regulating entity, then that entity —say a living cell—produces its own distinctive pulsating energy field; in fact it can be described *as* such. When billions of these cells join to form an enormously complex entity called a human being, a single, distinctive energy field is produced, which subsumes but is more than the sum of all the fields within.

Does what we call "matter" cause the energy fields, or do the energy fields cause the matter? Actually, matter *is* the energy field, as Einstein showed us in his equation, $E = mc^2$, and cause is not even involved. It is enough to say that rhythmic pattern is the most fundamental, irreducible aspect of any human being and that we can look at each of the markers of individuality as different manifestations of the same fundamental rhythm or inner pulse. Fingerprints, for example, are rhythmic waves frozen in space. Brainwaves are waves in time. We recognize a favorite singer, no matter what song is being sung, no matter how poor the electronic reproduction, not just through his or her interpretation of the song, but through this deeper rhythmic essence, this inner pulse. Researcher Manfred Clynes has detected and measured the inner pulse of the great classical composers: a sort of musical signature that somehow goes deeper than the notes of their music and that is passed down to us over the centuries.[1]

At essence, then, each of us can be thought of as an absolutely distinctive rhythmic field, a complex of waves and resonances. This concept of personal identity dissolves the ancient mind-body dichotomy, for the mind can be seen as one manifestation of the inner pulse, the body as another. We can go further and see a person's life work, the wake left in time by that person's passing, as a manifestation of this particular, fundamental pulse. The soul or spirit is another such manifestation. The idea of an inner pulse of personal identity points us toward an explanation of the possible survival of the distinctive self after the death of the body.

This formulation obviously can affect the context of erotic love. For me, in any case, it is wondrous indeed to perceive my lover as unique in all the universe, to know that every word between us, every glance, every touch is one of a kind, to realize that my experience of her is never to be repeated so long as time and space persist. An awesome thought! Yet there is something even more awesome for us to consider in the idea of *holonomy*.

From the earliest times, the human imagination has been haunted by a vision of universal connectedness, of all-in-oneness. The mystical tradition in every great religion— Hindu, Buddhist, Islamic, Jewish, or Christian—insists that every part of the universe in some sense contains the whole: the world in a grain of sand, as William Blake puts it. This vision goes back to primitive shamanism and forward to the thought of such philosophers as Spinoza, Leibnitz, and Whitehead.

And now modern science, once committed to the principle of rigorous separation, finds itself unexpectedly drawn towards the possibility of some kind of connection between everything in the universe. Many physicists are coming around to the point of view that there must be some significant influence between the observer and the observed, between consciousness and the environment. And physicist J. S. Bell, among others, maintains that any complete theory of reality must allow for the interconnectedness of distant events in a way that is contrary to everyday experience. Recent experiments tend to confirm Bell's thesis.[2]

But the most dramatic scientific model of interconnectedness, of all-in-oneness, is provided by holography, a form of photographic reproduction that uses no lenses. A hologram can be made by exposing negative film to intersecting light waves that are formed when laser light is split so that part of the laser beam goes directly to the film while the other part is bounced off an object, say a chair. When the film is developed, the resulting image looks nothing at all like a chair but rather like a smudgy collection of fingerprints. Then a beam of laser light is shone through the film, and an image of the chair is reconstructed, seeming to hang in midair in three dimensions.

A hologram is remarkable in many ways, but most remarkable is the fact that when the film is cut into two pieces, the entire picture can be reproduced from both pieces. No matter how many times the film is divided, in fact, each part can reproduce the whole image when illuminated by laser light. As the pieces get smaller, the image gets fuzzier. Photographic resolution is lost. *But the whole picture is there.* How can this be? Simply because every point on the film receives light from all parts of the object photographed, and contains, in encoded form, the entire image.

A hologram is a relatively simple thing: intersecting wave fronts of light captured on two-dimensional film. But it suggests a grander structure, a new way of seeing all the world. Brain researcher Karl Pribram of Stanford University, for example, has conducted experiments which suggest that information is distributed holonomically throughout the brain. And physicist David Bohm, of the University of London, takes the hologram as an analogy that suggests a radical new description of reality. He sees the universe as essentially a realm of frequencies and potentialities, with the objects of everyday existence making up a secondary order, a construct of human sensing. Pribram voices a tantalizing question, one that has occurred to many scientists in recent years: "What if the real world isn't made up of objects at all? What if *it's* a hologram?"

Further discussion of Pribram's question is beyond the scope of this exploration.[3] The mere fact that it is being asked gives currency to the ancient intuition of all-in-oneness. A hologram cannot explain the universe, but it gives us an idea of an overarching unity that expresses itself in every part, every aspect, of that unity—in every leaf, every blade of grass. From this, we might perceive the human individual as an integral piece of a universal whole. Just as a tiny fragment of a hologram contains the whole picture, a human individual might be said to "contain" the whole universe. In both cases, the picture lacks resolution. But somehow the whole structure is encoded in the human body and being. This implies that we have some sort of access to universal knowledge. How much of it we can bring to conscious awareness is, of course, limited—by the boundaries of our education, by the constraints of our social conditioning, by the capacity of our nervous system, by the structure of language itself.

But we have the *feel* of the universe, affirmed again and again by the intuition that we know more than we can say. The holonomic model might even explain certain putative paranormal phenomena. Holonomic knowing does not require a carrier wave (sound, light, radio, etc.) to get information from there to here, since universal information is built into the very structure of our being. We are not *in* but *of* the vast web of relationships that constitutes all of existence. We know something of distant events, distant worlds, because we are of them and they are of us.

Putting identity and holonomy together in a complementary relationship, we might be bold enough to perceive each human being as an entity that somehow both reflects and expresses the whole universe from a particular point of view. Such a perception can dramatically alter the erotic encounter, inviting us to experience the sacred, almost unimaginable potential that exists (whatever the outward imperfections) at the heart of every individual. It does not deny or ignore the existence of what we perceive as evil. The universal process involves destruction as well as construction, and all around us, if eyes can see and ears can hear, are flaws, imbalances, monstrosities. Thus, the perception of the person as the universe should in no way seduce us with foolish optimism or free us from the responsibility of choosing lovers prudently. But this perception finally liberates us from the chilling suspicion and fear that accompany purely negative views of the person and permits us wholehearted exploration of new worlds of love.

If both my love and I are fields of radiant energy, unique and irreducible, expressing the universe from particular points of view, then our joining is no casual matter. When the two of us come together in love, a new energy field is created, greater than and different from the sum of its parts. It too—this new entity made from the two of us—is unique and irreducible. It is new information in the universe. Because of our love, all existence has become richer. Here perhaps, in erotic joining, is creation's most compelling metaphor. No new physical life, no baby is necessary to make it real. Nor is it required that bodies be joined in physical love. Not even a touch is needed. Intentionality and commitment alone are enough to create new form, order where there was chaos or nothingness, new information. Even when we are worlds apart, the energy field that joins us persists, more powerful, as the poets have always said, than stone walls, iron bars, wind and waves.

When I approach my love as the universe, there is no way I can treat her as an object. It is easy to forget the true nature of our relationship, to take miracles for granted. But sometimes, even in the most ordinary circumstances of daily life—shopping for groceries, washing dishes—I am overcome with a sense of awe. Through her, I have found a new window to the universe. The stuff of the senses is transformed: clouds and trees, cars, and buildings reveal their inner rhythms. The vise of space, time, and momentum eases its grip on my imagination, and I realize that miracles happen all the time; it's just that we don't acknowledge them.

Make no mistake, the universe that opens through our relationship is not made altogether of sweetness and light, but rather is pregnant with mystery and surprise: enormous clouds of darkness, exploding galaxies, matter and anti-matter, even what seems most substantial collapsing in on itself and disappearing. When we make love, I am offered an erotic representation of all of this: the violence and repose, the agreeable terror, the destruction and subsequent reassertion of self. A lifetime is too short to explore all that is available to the two of us.

I think this is what Buber means by I-Thou. This is what calls most of us, what we yearn for even as we race from bed to bed, shirttails aflame, reciting our list of conquests. This is High Monogamy, love that remains fresh and new as it deepens and matures.

An Uncommon Option

High Monogamy is not for everyone, nor is it the only path to creative, transformative love. Sometimes the most fleeting erotic encounter can strike the chord of poignancy and delight that has the power to transform lives, and in youth a certain amount of erotic exploration is a natural urge. High Monogamy deserves a brief discussion here simply because, in an age that is fascinated with erotic options, it is one option that is rarely mentioned. I define it as a long-term relationship in which both members are *voluntarily* committed to erotic exclusivity, not because of legal, moral or religious scruples, not because of timidity or inertia, *but because they seek challenge and an adventure*.

High Monogamy requires, first of all, a goodly supply of self-esteem in both partners. Psychologist Nathaniel Branden, one of the rare modern writers who advocates romantic love, argues that no other factor is more important.

It has become something of a cliché to observe that, if we do not love ourselves, we cannot love anyone else. This is true enough, but it is only part of the picture. If we do not love ourselves, it is almost impossible to believe fully that we *are loved* by someone else. It is almost impossible to *accept* love. It is almost impossible to *receive* love. No matter what our partner does to show that he or she cares, we do not experience the devotion as convincing because we do not feel lovable to ourselves.[4]

Self-esteem, no matter how important, is not all that is required of those who would take the path of High Monogamy. It is essential that both partners have mutual interests and share a common vision of life's purpose and how to achieve it. Each partner needs the ability to celebrate and support the other, not only in low moments but also in high. "Never marry a person," Nathaniel Branden tells his clients, "who is not a friend of your excitement." The High Monogamist is not blindly approving but rather is dedicated to an uncommon openness and honesty. At the same time, he or she knows *how* to be open and honest without being abrasive or dogmatic.

Some of the virtues needed for High Monogamy—such things as enthusiasm, loyalty, courtesy, and patience—have become so platitudinous as to fade into the background noise of the modern world. And yet, unacknowledged, their presence or absence shapes the outcome of every relationship. In a book on marriage,[5] the great psychologist Carl Rogers tells us that when he turned forty he mysteriously became impotent. This condition lasted a year, during which his wife remained cheerful, loving, and supportive. At the end of the year, his impotence disappeared, never to return. His wife's uncanny patience so touched Rogers that he knew he would love her until the end of her days.

Still, it is not merely the exercise of the common virtues that marks the High Monogamist, but rather a sort of towering, vertiginous daring. For this state requires that we look directly and unflinchingly at our every weakness and flaw, straight down through layer after layer of cowardice and self-deception to the very heart of our intentionality. And in High Monogamy we are forced, as well, to confront something even more terrifying: our beauty and magnificence, our potential to love and create and feel deeply, and the daily, hourly, moment-by-moment waste of that potential. And when we achieve the unnerving clarity that High Monogamy demands, we must either beat a fast retreat or undertake to transform ourselves.

Simone de Beauvoir has argued that eroticism "is a movement toward the *Other*, this is its essential character, but in the deep intimacy of the couple, husband and wife become for one another the *Same*; no exchange is any longer possible, no giving and no conquering."[6] De Beauvoir in this case failed to look deeply enough into the possibilities of the monogamous situation. High Monogamy is not a mere fusion, not a mutual loss of self. It is the reassertion of a more fundamental self, explainable only through paradox: *The more I am truly myself, the more I can be truly one with you. The more I am truly one with you, the more I can be truly myself.* The paradox is inescapable. In High Monogamy, the couple constitutes a single entity made of two autonomous entities. For each person, the partner is both the Same *and* the Other. In this regard, the couple models the ancient mystery of multiplicity within unity, identity within holonomy.

It is easy to associate multiple sexual partners with personal change and monogamy with personal stasis. This can at times be true; after years of the stultification of what might be called Low Monogamy, having an affair can reawaken dulled perceptions and trigger a transformation of sorts. But extramarital affairs or the pursuit of recreational sex are far more likely to be associated with the avoidance of change. After superficial erotic novelty has faded, after ego has had its full run (all the life stories told, all the sexual tricks displayed), *then* the adventure of transformation and a deeper eroticism can begin. But it is precisely at this point that most of us are likely to lose our nerve and leap into another bed, where we can once again tell our stories, display our tricks, do *anything* rather than see ourselves clearly and start doing something about it.

Indeed, one glimpse into the powerful mirror of High Monogamy might be all it takes to send us back into the desolate comfort of Low Monogamy or out in hot pursuit of the-same-thing-another-time-around. In either case, the underlying, unacknowledged aim is to avoid change, to be allowed to lead an essentially predictable life. High Monogamy, merciless in its presentation of self-knowledge, demands that we change, that we have the courage to lead an essentially unpredictable life.

Advocates of multiple sex have a saying: "Why should I be satisfied with a sandwich when there's a feast out there?" Obviously, they have never experienced High Monogamy. Those of us who have tried both tend to see it differently. Casual recreational sex is hardly a feast—not even a good, hearty sandwich. It is a diet of fast food served in plastic containers. Life's feast is available only to those who are willing and able to engage life on a deeply personal level, giving all, holding back nothing.

It would be a mistake to overpraise High Monogamy. Nothing is quite as glorious as it can be made to sound, and human beings are ingenious in discovering ways to sabotage their own joy. Still, for those adventurers who can make the leap into commitment, the rewards are great: a rare tenderness, an exaltation, a highly charged erotic ambience, surprise on a daily basis, transformation. But there is no insurance policy.

No wonder High Monogamy is so rare and so rarely even mentioned. The survey takers, in fact, suggest that it is virtually impossible. Romance fades, they proclaim, after an average of fifteen months. Or is it eighteen months, or three years? In any case, romance fades. And they are often right.

Civilization has trained us well in restlessness and manipulation. To be prepared for civilization's work of building and doing, of conquest and exploitation, it is best to be somewhat uneasy in our skins, dissatisfied with the present moment. Romance seems merely palliative. Dis-ease is habitual. We fall out of the present. We forget our lover is the universe. Glancing anxiously at the past and the future, we resort to calculation. Our lover becomes, again, an object, an *It*. Ignoring our heart's desire, we conclude the survey takers are right. For most of us, High Monogamy remains a condition to be realized, difficult to describe, much less achieve. Its converse is easy:

We dedicate ourselves to job, school, politics, golf. We let love take care of itself. What happens? A joining that begins in passion relapses into cliché while the first fresh taste of love is still on your lips. The moment comes (too soon!) when you run across tax forms among old love letters. "Notice of Adjustment. Part I—Tax-Payer's Copy." And suddenly, Sunday finds you sprawled not on that high, singing meadow where the eyes of your love were able somehow to hold the universe but in front of the TV. After six hours of pro football, the most brilliantly executed fake buck and roll-out seems trivial; the beer tastes like used detergent; the peanuts lie like hot mud at the bottom of your belly. Your love walks by, and a mechanical hand (one of yours?) reaches up to pat her on the fanny. As for her, she shakes her head and moves to check the washing machine. The machine churns in the background. Everything is secure. But your love isn't there. Her mind has flown her to that faraway sea of poppies on the edge of the cornfield where she is saying over and over, as did Madame Bovary, "O God, O God, why did I get married?"[6]

And yet the dream persists. We look at those rare couples who are still mad for each other after twenty years of marriage, who embarrass us with their dinner party embraces, as somehow freakish, exceptions who prove the rule. Still, we envy them. In spite of surveys, hard experience and Sexual Revolution dogma, we launch ourselves again and again toward surrender and commitment. Some subterranean impulse draws us into romance even when it is unfashionable.

The cynic's wisdom has a long pedigree. Perhaps we would be wise to settle for healthy sensuality, recreational sex. I-Thou relationships are risky; commitment is scary. Perceiving our lover as the universe can lead to unrealistic expectations and thus to hurt and disillusionment. So we may choose to be "realistic," to lower our expectations, to go on making the sort of half-hearted, calculated commitment that so often leads to Skinnerian entrapment, then to infidelity or open marriage. Or maybe we're willing, from the beginning, to settle for creature comforts, parallel play, companionate love. Maybe it is irresponsible to push anyone toward the terrors of total commitment.

But there is also something terrifying about the waste of potential. This life is as sharp as the edge of a sword between an eternity behind us and an eternity ahead. Perhaps the cut is clean and true only when, on certain fine occasions, we give all of ourselves, relinquishing all expectations, judgement, and considered opinion, living bravely in the eternal moment. We cannot make that cut through abstraction, generalization, classification, and categorization—those sometimes-useful tools of civilization are the enemies of love and creation—but only through a repersonalization of all of life. Habits can take weeks, months, or years to turn around, but perceptions can change in an instant. New perceptions are prerequisite for all significant change, providing both guidance and impetus for the process of transformation that follows.

We begin, as I have said, by seeing the human individual as a vibrant and unique field of energy, as a window into the universe, even as the universe itself. This radical repersonalization is by no means the exclusive prerogative of those who are dedicated to High Monogamy, who are fortunate enough to have found their longtime mates. It is also possible, as I've suggested, in an erotic encounter that lasts only a few brief hours. All truly erotic love involves two vibrant entities merging to become a new vibrancy, something truly novel in the universe. And when love ends, something of that vibrancy remains, some enrichment of all of existence.

No act of love is intrinsically trivial. We have been carefully taught in countless covert ways to make it so. But at every instant a choice remains: to perceive anew, to brush the cobwebs of custom from our eyes, to surrender to the dangerous destiny of truly personal love.

CHAPTER THIRTEEN

A Body of Love

THE HUMAN BODY has been seen as a fortress, a machine, a container of life and consciousness, and an obdurate, immoral mass of flesh. Let me offer a different view: the body as an opening, a metaphor, and a teacher—a body of love.

The Body as an Opening

In the preceding chapter, I presented a way of seeing the self as essentially a wave form. The body, in this view, is one manifestation of that wave form. It is the self's way of opening out to the universe of three dimensions, of gravity and momentum. The body is by no means a mere object, a fortress walled off from the outer environment by the skin and guarded by sensory sentinels, but rather it is an integral part of the environment, continually exchanging energy and information with its surroundings.

Most of the time, the body's relationships with the environment are marked by a degree of harmony that is truly remarkable. The body continually takes in heat and gives off heat, and yet the internal temperature generally varies by only a few percentage points. The chemical balance of the blood—its salinity, for example—maintains itself within an equally exquisite range. The body's most fundamental interactions with the environment—breathing, drinking, eating, excreting—are interactions of accommodation and balance, not warfare. Bacteria and viruses flow in and out of the body, in most cases friends rather than enemies of human life and health.

Within stability, there is always change. Every seven years, on the average, every cell in the body is replaced. Every few months, all body proteins are replaced. Every few days, the epidermal layer of the skin is replaced. Every second, approximately 2.5 million red blood cells die; at the same time, some 2.5 million new cells are born. The body is more like a flame than a lump of clay, continually burning yet not consumed. The substance of which it is made changes. The form, the wave in space and time, persists.

Even the body's apparent solidity is an illusion, perpetuated by the limited range of visual sensitivity. The body is opaque to a narrow band of the electromagnetic spectrum, mostly to what we recognize as visible light. But light occupies just one octave of some seventy in the full spectrum, and the body is translucent or transparent to almost all of this energy—heat, X rays, radio waves, gamma rays. If we could take an incredible voyage into the body, becoming smaller and smaller as we entered cells, components of cells, molecules, atoms, and finally the vibrant heart of the atom itself, we would find no static substance at all, only pattern and pulse: emptiness and a dance.

Just in physical terms, the body is one of those forms of nature that are called *open systems*. The Belgian physical chemist Ilya Prigogene, who won the 1977 Nobel Prize for chemistry, has developed a theory to explain the behavior of such systems, which he terms "dissipative structures." (The term derives from the fact that the system maintains its form by continually taking in and dissipating energy.)

The continual flow of energy creates fluctuations, which the system counterbalances in the process of maintaining its integrity. But when the fluctuations reach a certain critical point, they "perturb" the system. If the perturbations are too great, the system cannot survive. Within a reasonable limit, however, the perturbations create the possibility of transformation, increasing the number of novel interactions within the system, creating new connections, causing a reorganization of the system into a higher order.[1]

The process of physical conditioning provides a clear example. Take a runner who has achieved a certain level of speed and endurance and who wants to reach a higher level. Improvement will probably not come easily. Homeostasis, the tendency of any self-regulating system to maintain itself in its current state, resists change for the better as well as change for the worse. The runner's attempts to reach a new level of performance will be accompanied by significant perturbations within the body, variously sensed as pain, anxiety, confusion, or even fear of death. Clearly, the system is being shaken up. But, if the runner persists, there generally comes a moment of reordering, a transformation, when everything within the body seems suddenly to fall into place, producing a new homeostasis at a higher level and better performance on the track.

The act of love presents a more striking example, even when we view it (as much as is possible) in terms of the body alone. In this act, as we saw in Part I, the body of each lover undergoes dramatic perturbations. Muscles rhythmically convulse. Air rushes in and out of the lungs. The cardiovascular system is driven to its limit. Liquid pours from the sweat glands and mucous membranes. Body contours are altered. Urgent hormonal and neuronal messages race throughout the body. Just as the telephone system is jammed during an emergency, the body's information circuits are overloaded. This information overload, in fact, starts blanking out the senses of sight, hearing, smell, taste and touch, leading, at the point of orgasm, to a kind of ecstatic unconsciousness: *la petite mort*.

Is all this bodily perturbation needed for the expression of Eros? Not necessarily. The self, that essential underlying wave form, is called to love through resonance with another self; there can be erotic love without even the touching of hands. But, as poet Abraham Cowley put it,

> *Indeed I must confess,*
> *When souls mix, 'tis an happiness;*
> *But not complete till bodies too combine. . . .*

The body opens each lover to the other, offers the two of them together the chance to reenact the myth of creation, to somehow become, if only for a little while, a single organism; something new in the universe. The act of love is a crisis, a time of danger and opportunity. The overload of energy and information is so great (taking the two bodies as one system now) that new connections must be made, through touch or speech or the invisible bonds of a deepened empathy, to keep the system from flying apart. In this as in all systems, rhythm serves the function of organization. True lovers move in synchrony, breathe together. Their words and cries accompany their movements; two pendulums of passion swing as one. Rape of any type or degree is irredeemably unerotic precisely because it is not synchronous. But when the fierce rhythms of bodily love pulse together, wonders can occur. The dramatic perturbations within the system produce a reordering, a transformation. Trivial distinctions are blurred, and larger connections become possible—with nature, with others. The body provides an opening to the physical universe. Two bodies as one provide an opening of a higher order.

The Body as Metaphor

Far from opposing the will of the mind and spirit, the body replicates it with amazing fidelity. A person's body—not necessarily the outer shape of it but the way it is held and used —generally offers us a clear representation of how that person lives.

These statements might seem so obvious as to need no further elaboration. But we of this culture have been so relentlessly programmed to believe the body is separate from and opposed to the mind and spirit that what might seem obvious is often most difficult to grasp. Since 1973, I have introduced a practice called Energy Training to more than 35,000 people from many different walks of life. This work comes from the sophisticated and nonaggressive martial art of aikido. One of its principles is that the body can serve as a metaphor for everything else in life. Many of the people who attend the workshops are intellectually committed to that very principle. Yet it is not at all uncommon, two or three hours into the first session, for someone to comment that he or she can't understand the connection between a rigidly held arm and rigid child-rearing practices or a rigid philosophy. This resistance to understanding persists in spite of numerous books on "body language," in spite of the fact that body metaphors are deeply embedded in common discourse: brokenhearted, thin-skinned, tight-assed, pain in the neck, head of the company, ahead of yourself, get off my back, make a clean breast of it.

The truth of the matter is that once you've shaken hands with someone, you've already gained a certain amount of information on how that person lives and relates with others. A few minutes of close dancing provides a fairly reliable preview of lovemaking. Muggers choose their victims, according to a recent study at Rahway State Penitentiary in New Jersey, by the way they walk.[2] The messages of the body are indeed profound. We rely on these messages all the time, often on a subconscious level. We fail to credit them or even bring them to conscious awareness to the extent that we have internalized the mind-body dualism of our culture.

At the simplest level, metaphor is a way of using something already understood to explain something not so well understood. Sir Walter Raleigh writes:

> *But true love is a durable fire*
> *In the mind ever burning,*
> *Never sick, never old, never dead,*
> *From itself never turning.*

He assumes that we understand the nature of a durable, constantly burning fire and that through this understanding we can come to know more about true love.

But metaphor is not merely a poetic device. Ultimately, it is pervasive. If only we could go back far enough, linguists tell us, we would find that language is an unbroken web, spun strand by strand through one thing's standing for another, standing for yet another. Every word is a buried metaphor, and the primordial words probably had to do with body and bodily function—hunger, thirst, pain, danger, love —grunts and cries made articulate.

Metaphor is connection, and it is also metamorphosis, transformation. We see this in the Christian doctrine of transubstantiation. The bread and wine of the Mass do not simply *stand for* the body and blood of Christ, they *become* it. Bread and wine *are* body and blood. What is veiled in discourse is revealed in poetry; all language, all existence, is transubstantive. The verb *is*, explicit and implicit, is the most erotic of words—joining, then transforming, the world of things and events; and finally, in the key phrase of Eastern religion, *Tat tvan asi* "That art thou," dissolving all distinctions in a mystical oneness.

Metaphor is magic, but it loses its power to transform when distinctions are erased, when metamorphosis is detached from its physical, bodily foundations. Northrop Frye, writing of William Blake's vision, points out that the real apocalypse—the word means literally to uncover or discover —"comes, not with the vision of a city or kingdom, which would still be external, but with the identification of the city and kingdom with one's own body."[3] The Word in stories of creation does not echo soundlessly in the void, but brings a physical world into being. (*"Earth! they said, and instantly it was made."*) It is the Word incarnate that has the power to transform existence.

The religious and philosophical neglect or denigration of the body represents a fundamental Western heresy. In our haste to dominate the world through abstraction and generalization, we of the West seem to have forgotten that all language and thought, even that which we now so carelessly abstract, had its genesis in the body. We have attempted to vacate the body, so much so that bodily maladies can develop and run wild for months without the conscious knowledge of the imperial mind. (In this disembodied way of living, sickness is somehow separate from the self, just as "sex" is, a matter for professionals to deal with from the outside.) But now, especially in the United States, our attitude toward the body is undergoing a transformation. Many millions of people here are well into the process of reinhabiting their bodies and finding out—an ancient truth rediscovered —how much the body can tell.

When I reinhabit my body and become aware of bodily balance and imbalance, I gain first-hand knowledge about all balance and imbalance—of things and events and ideas. When I pay the price of rigidity in my body, I realize its price in the world. From this bodily learning, I may come to experience the true suppleness that engenders power and inhibits violence. The dangers of over-reaching are clear in the body, and in the world. A balanced, centered way of walking models a way of moving a society. In the body and the body politic, anxiety binds energy, while arousal releases it. (Many of us have been anxious so long that we have forgotten what it is like to be simply and joyfully aroused to action.)

Bodily metaphor is even more poignant in the realm of Eros. The body's curves and planes become all curves and planes. Every true lover is an explorer, every act of true love an exploration. In John Donne's words:

> License my roaving hands, and let them go,
> Before, behind, between, above, below.
> O my America! my new-found-land,
> My kingdome, safeliest when with one man man'd,
> My Myne of precious stone, My Emperie,
> How blest am I in this discovering thee!

Form and function as metaphor: the female breasts themselves, not words, stand, more than for motherhood, for all burgeoning, all blossoming, nature's generosity. And in the pelvis, female and male, we see the fundamental, rhythmic power of all generation, along with the paradoxical relationship between creation and decay: love, as Yeats reminds us, "has pitched his mansion in / The place of excrement."

Do words shape or simply reflect the world? Is the penis a rod, a tool, an avenger—or is it a tower, a totem, a god? You can choose: language creates reality creates language. Is the vagina a box, a purse, a snatch—or is it a vortex of mysteries, a passageway into endless summer? Choose again: experience creates words creates experience. Is every erection, as St. Augustine would have it, an insurrection of the flesh—or is it an emblem of creation, a precursor of new information, news from the universe? The truth is held in words but springs from a deeper source: the primordial experience of opening to the space-time world *as a body*, itself a manifestation of an even more elemental inner pulse.

Do you experience erotic sensation throughout the whole body or only in the genitals? The question is far from trivial. "Genitality" or "genital organization," according to Freud, is a well-organized tyranny of one part of the body over the whole of the body. It is the bodily manifestation of "sex." Norman O. Brown takes psychoanalysis a step further, equating genitality with monarchy or any kind of capital organization. The penis as "head" of the body, Brown argues, is the erotic equivalent of the head itself as the "head" of the body. In this regard, genitals and cerebrum are essentially the same, both of them tyrants.[4] One who suffers this tyranny in the body is well prepared to endure or impose a similar tyranny in the world. Whole-body eroticism, on the other hand, suggests a more collaborative community, empathic governance, a use of power not according to Hobbes but of Blake, who had strong feelings on this matter.

Embraces are Cominglings from the head even to the feet,
And not a pompous High Priest entering by a Secret Place.

When I join your body, I participate in all joining. I join all of me with all of you. Your body is not an object. My body is not an instrument. We join in full awareness, fully responsible, willing to endure times of separation and waiting, false starts, aimless play, foolishness, vulnerability, strenuous effort, total surrender. In that joining is ecstasy and sadness (it can't last forever; it must end) and also transformation: the creation of a new whole greater than the sum of its parts, an opening to deeper mysteries.

The mystery cannot be denied. To demystify the erotic is not merely to trivialize but to falsify it. Take the metaphor involved in veiling and unveiling, covering and uncovering the body. Nudists are right in claiming their practice is nonsexual. As a veteran of many years of mixed nudity in hot baths, I have finally concluded that the practice is generally anti-erotic, and indeed, forgive me, companions of the baths, a mild perversion of the erotic potential. I recall a friend who lived for weeks in dread of entering mixed hot baths, an action he felt compelled to take in pursuit of a journalistic assignment, for he was sure he would get an erection. When it turned out that he didn't and, in fact, was not in the least aroused, his reaction was relief mixed with mild disappointment.

Here is ideology again. According to the ideologists, public nudity is *supposed* to be natural and freeing. It isn't. Far from being natural, in fact, nonerotic nudity in large mixed groups is quite unnatural. Few indeed are the cultures, no matter how primitive, in which there is no clothing whatever. Body covering is not merely an ornament or a protection from the elements, but rather a metaphor of the mystery of generation. Uncovering is discovering; unveiling the body stands for all unveiling. To reserve full nakedness for the personal erotic encounter is to enhance both nakedness and the erotic, as poets and lovers have always known. John Donne again:

> Like pictures, or like books gay coverings made
> For lay-men, are all women thus array'd;
> Themselves are mystick books, which only wee
> (Whom their imputed grace will dignifie)
> Must see reveal'd.

Row upon row of naked bodies denies the mystery and serves ultimately as yet another depersonalization. In the mass, bodies become increasingly abstract and general. Distinctions become merely anatomical. A peculiar, somewhat strained code of conduct belies the ideologists' "freedom." Though massages might be acceptable, other forms of intimate touch definitely are not; there are more embraces at a cocktail party. Once I was present when a beautiful woman entered the baths wearing only a string of pearls. The effect was electrifying and quite erotic.

I think I would prefer baths where a certain mild arousal would be recognized as natural, where it would be all right to look openly at the entire body rather than quickly averting the eyes after a surreptitious glance at the genital area. Those surreptitious glances, those short-circuited arousals, stand for the strange sort of lie involved in all current attempts to trivialize and demystify the erotic. The mythic truth outlives the lie, the ancient myth of discovery, of fully erotic nakedness, reenacted again and again in the veiling and unveiling of the body: flesh-and-blood metaphor of all mystery.

The Body as Teacher

The builders of teaching machines tend to overlook the best learning facility of all. The body is fully instrumented. It has thousands of feedback circuits. And the feedback is instantaneous. The body contains more information than all the libraries in the world, for it codifies, in its structure and its genes, evolutionary experience that goes all the way back to the first living organism. At the microscopic and submicroscopic levels, the body holds even more information: a catalog of crystals, complex molecules, simple molecules, heavy atoms, light atoms, ionized particles, and quanta of pure energy that link the time-and-space self to the birth of the universe, when time and space themselves were born. The body, in Michael Murphy's words, is all time remembered. Written into each body, moreover, in its posture, its habitual responses, its very tissue and veins, is a clear record of the particulars of that life.

When we vacate our bodies, splitting intellect from flesh, this vast store of information is unavailable to us. When we reinhabit the body and learn to understand its messages, we gain access to a treasury of knowledge and guidance.

One obstacle to bodily knowledge is overreliance on our eyes. The sharply focussed, linear picture of the environment that we gain through vision is rich in information. But if the eyes inform, they also mislead. At the most fundamental level, the universe is lensless or, if you will, holonomic. Alfred North Whitehead is one of the few Western thinkers who have recognized the importance of the body in perception. "Philosophers," he writes, "have disdained the information about the universe obtained through their visceral feelings, and have concentrated on visual feelings."[5] Sometimes, indeed, we can learn more of the universe in darkness than in light. In Rilke's words:

You darkness, that I come from,
I love you more than all the fires
that fence in the world,
for the fire makes
a circle of light for everyone,
and then no one outside learns of you.

But the darkness pulls in everything:
shapes and fires, animals and myself,
how easily it gathers them!—
powers and people—

and it is possible a great energy
is moving near me.

I have faith in nights.

In darkness, horizons dissolve. Time turns fluid. Space be-comes indefinite; the self may be experienced (as medieval philosophers said of God) as a sphere whose center is every-where and whose circumference is nowhere. The first in-struction in many consciousness-altering exercises is simply "close your eyes." We have discovered in Energy Training workshops that groups of people, walking randomly with eyes closed, can experience a large room as infinite space. Within that space, they can take symbolic journeys, have adventures, endure ordeals, and seek new visions in the darkness.

There is also an alternate way of seeing we call "soft eyes," which gives access to bodily knowledge. This involves not *reaching out* with the eyes but *letting* the world come in; the eyes are open but focussed on nothing in particular. With soft eyes, peripheral vision is markedly increased, col-ors often appear more vivid, and the ability to see relation-ships among all things within the visual field is greatly enhanced. Brainwave measurements suggest that with soft eyes, the verbal, rational left hemisphere of the brain goes into a sort of idle speed, giving dominance to the intuitive, pattern-recognizing right hemisphere. The soft-eyed state is often associated with extraordinary perceptual and athletic feats.

Tuning into the body may start with closed or soft eyes or take place in darkness. But these limitations on the visual are not required. What is most needed is the simple assumption that bodily movements can inform and that there is wisdom in the flesh. We might bear in mind that some of Einstein's most important theories, as he himself explained, began with feelings in his muscles. Bodily knowledge can be of benefit in creative problem solving, in memory work, in improving relationships, in every aspect of life.

A certain humility is also required. This culture has put much emphasis on "mastering the body," and it is obvious that a great deal of disciplined practice is crucial in sports and the bodily arts. To transcend the commonplace, it is equally crucial, once basic mastery is achieved, to approach the body as a student, not as a master. Humbly attending to instructions from the teacher within, we are privy to the kind of guidance and grace that makes a great dancer or athlete. More than just that, the body offers guidance in everything that is human.

This is especially true in the erotic realm. For example, one of the more conspicuous frauds perpetrated on the erotically ignorant and needy is that ecstasy can come from forcing the body into a wide variety of exotic physical positions. To know that such variety is possible and permissible is well and good. But real joy can come only from turning off the imperial mind and putting aside all its sharply focused pictures. Erotic images can excite erotic feelings, but it is significant that the process of arousal involves progressively softer eyes and often leads us down through an interior darkness where eyes are of no use at all. The preconceived "positions" of the sex books serve essentially to illustrate all that is studied and limited in "sex." What Whitehead calls "visceral feeling," on the other hand, is always in the moment, thus always spontaneous, always nonlinear and unbounded, thus infinitely creative. In this lensless realm, stereotypes cannot exist. Manipulations become impossible. The teacher within insists upon I-Thou relationships.

Indeed, the body's ability to find the way of connectedness and harmony with another's body is truly astounding. William F. Condon's frame-by-frame analyses of bodily micromovements show that during any conversation both speaker and listener are entrained with one another down to the last syllable and subsyllable of speech, moving together in a dance too swift and subtle for the naked eye to see. Other studies suggest that something as simple as reading aloud together can bring two or more peoples' breathing, heartbeat, and even brainwaves into synchrony. But talking and reading aloud provide only elementary examples of how bodies can join at levels deeper than thought. The process of erotic arousal provides nearly infinite opportunities for this preverbal connectedness.

Tuning into another's body, becoming one with another being, starts with tuning into your own body. Once you learn to pay attention to messages from within, you quickly discover that bodily messages can freely pass between yourself and another and that the miracle of synchrony can occur. Wise lovers know how to talk with one another, to ask clearly for what they want (but not to demand that their requests be fulfilled), and to report clearly on what feels good or not so good. But when the rhythms of love take command, words become superfluous. Two bodies in communion need no book of instructions. Hands and lips know where to go and when. No grand strategy, no set of tactics are needed; plans and programs fly out the window. Every movement, every sensation, is new. The theme, the physical configuration of the act, might seem familiar, but the variations are endless. In this respect, everyone is potentially a creative genius, a Mozart of love.

When the body is teacher, we also see "impotence" and "frigidity" in a new light, not necessarily as maladies to be cured or problems to be solved, but rather as messages to be heeded. It must be said that some genital malfunctions are caused by purely physiological defects that might be remedied by medical measures and that some deep-seated cases of impotence or frigidity might be amenable to the programs developed by sex therapists. But most cases are simply statements by the body that sexual intercourse at this time and place, under these conditions, in this relationship, is inappropriate.

The genitals often are compelled to speak in lieu of some resentment unspoken or some other important information withheld. Techniques for forcing the genitals to operate against their own better judgement might bring the same kind of "fast, temporary relief" promised by various nonprescription drugs. In the long run, however, the situation can only worsen. To ignore or countermand the teacher within us is to deaden the emotions, to dam the flow of feelings, to armor the body and the self against itself. It is significant that responsible therapists warn clients who plan to enter sex therapy that if the therapy succeeds, their relationship may well fly apart. Even when tricked into potency, the body eventually has its way.

But what is this compulsion to force the body to perform some sort of "sex," against its will? Better to accept the wisdom of the genitals, to seek the hidden cause, to change your life. Most of all, not to get stuck on the *idea* of failure. (One of the sexologists' cruelest dogmas, often pressed on the aging, is "Use it or lose it.") The teacher within is no ideologist. Its message acknowledged, it can respond in an instant.

A man who has been deceiving his wife while on business trips begins having trouble getting erections, not just with his wife, but with his mistress as well. At last, he confesses all to his wife. Almost immediately, his genitals are fully responsive, whether or not his wife accepts the confession, whether or not he ceases his affair. The point in this particular case is that the body does not demand adherence to any particular moral code, only to a certain acknowledgement of the truth.

"In the depths," Rilke writes, "all becomes law." The body, manifesting the essential wave form that makes each of us unique in all the universe, responds unerringly to another being, another essential wave form, with which it resonates. "Love at first sight" might turn out wrong in a moral sense or disastrous in a practical sense, but it is not trivial. What we call "chemistry" is by no means a sufficient condition for a successful long-term relationship; habits, common interests, finances, careers, ability to communicate and other such matters must also be considered. But it is a necessary condition. To ignore this deeper resonance in favor of some image, some picture, or some idea is to discount the creative urge from which life itself springs.

"Like a thunderbolt." "Swept away." "Something bigger than both of us." Every cliché applies when we fall deeply in love. It is a recognition, a rejoining of some lost part of ourselves, a miracle. We must have known each other before, in some past life. No wonder lovers so often turn to reincarnation as an explanation of the power and inevitability of their attraction.

If not past lives, then what? Prescientific explanations— possession, Cupid's dart, love potions—might now seem naive. But they encode information in symbolic form that our present science fails to take into account. The tragic power of a forbidden romance is noise in the system of the sexologists. Yet a story such as that of Tristan and Iseult moves us in a way that recreational sex never can and never will. When Iseult drank a love potion, thinking it was wine, the author tells us that

Now she had found not wine—but Passion and Joy most sharp, and Anguish without end, and Death.

And when Tristan also drank and felt the effects of the potion, it was as if an ardent briar, sharp-thorned but with flower most sweet smelling, drave roots into his blood and laced the lovely body of Iseult all round about it and bound it to his own and to his every thought and desire.[6]

What extravagant language! We have been taught to beware of such romantic passion or, better yet, to ridicule it. After all, someone might get hurt. Recreational sex (forget the VD) is far safer. According to the insurance mentality that currently prevails, life should be totally safe and successful for everybody; all risk should be minimized. In the erotic realm, this mentality produces a curious trade-off: while libido is liberated (in the service of commerce as well as pleasure, it must be said), passionate, committed love is repressed.

But what is repressed is not buried. The desire for commitment is there in the body, whether heeded or ignored. If we have vacated the body, if we fail to get the message straight and clear, we are sure to get it other ways: senses deadened, muscles armored, restlessness, anxiety, inexplicable sickness. The unwillingness to risk loss and pain results in loss and pain. Tristan's experience is not just symbol; it is bodily knowledge. Have you never felt that way—your lover's body laced around your own, rooted like briars in your blood? There is no policy I know of that can insure the body against the pain of true passion or buy you truly committed love without risk and eventual loss.

For my part, I would choose commitment and passion, knowing the risks, willing to feel the pain. It has taken a few years, but my body has finally shown me the enormous lie in some of the cherished dogmas of the Sexual Revolution: of personal love without jealousy, sensual pleasure without consequences, recreation without creation. I know now that without the possibility of defeat, no victory can be so full and fine, that without the possibility of tragedy, no love can be so rich and keen. Now I understand the catch in the throat at the moment of surrender, the throb of sadness at the height of orgasm, the unexpected tears at a wedding. For fully committed lovers, a sense of tragedy is a valued gift. To deny it is to lose life's savor.

"Till death do we part" is the key phrase in almost every ceremony of commitment. In that phrase lies the body's ultimate teaching, written in its every gene: that we must die. The truth is clear. This body that has opened me to the universe of time and space and momentum will close that particular opening. This body that has joined me to my love will sever that particular connection. There may well be other openings, other connections. "Forever" may well imply other explorations. But that does not soften the tragedy. On this plane of existence, what I most love I must lose. Shall I, then, love less? How I answer that question, not just verbally but at the deepest level of my being, determines the quality of my love.

CHAPTER FOURTEEN

An Erotic Society

In the preceding chapters, I've proposed that our view of the person and of the body strongly affects our erotic experience. The converse also holds: our erotic experience strongly affects the way we view the person and the body. This is also true of our approach to the outside world. For example, a person who believes wholeheartedly that "winning isn't everything, it's the only thing" is likely to approach every erotic encounter as a contest. This equation can be turned around: the person who makes love to win is likely to be highly competitive in other matters as well.

In Chapter Nine, we saw Norman Mailer's fictional persona engaged in a grueling, three-night-long contest for what he considered sexual victory. Mailer, to recapitulate, is quite clear about the relationship between this contest and the rest of life. "I had won," he tells us. "At no matter what cost, and with what luck, and with a piece of charity from her, I had won nonetheless, and since all real pay came from victory, it was more likely that I would win the next time I gambled my stake on something more appropriate for my ambition."

Mailer's clarity is helpful. For if all real pay comes from victory, if there must be winners and losers, if winning can be as abstract as numbers on a scoreboard or as hollow as the dying cry of "Victory" from the one survivor in a heap of rubble and corpses—if indeed this is the real and only world in which we can live—then erotic tenderness and surrender must be seen as inappropriate, a threat to survival itself. The unceasing desire for "Power after power," as Hobbes reminds us, stems from fear, and those who are most caught up in the quest for power over others are likely to have sex lives as bizarre as the marriage between domination and terror. For some power seekers, the strategies and manipulations and the force majeure of the boardroom are simply transferred to the bedroom; sex becomes domination. For others, there is a flip-flop, a change of sign from plus to minus, and we have the picture of a steely-eyed corporation executive or a cigar-smoking political boss asking to be tied down, whipped, humiliated. Through this action, it would seem, some imbalance in the world is righted. But in either case, whether through the direct assertion of power over others or through role reversal, there is a clear relationship between private and public behavior, between the erotic and the world.

To the extent that we buy into a society that values and engenders manipulation, acquisition, competition, and the exploitation of nature and other people, our erotic experience is likely to be limited, no matter how sexually liberated we may be. To the extent that we abstract and depersonalize our public lives, we are likely to have difficulty in relating person to person, heart to heart, in our private lives.

Sexual liberation, as we have seen, is not enough. People are still looking for passion and commitment, for those magical moments that seem to join us with the process of creation itself. The moments exist, but for most of us in this culture, they are rare, often coming when least expected, holding out the promise of deliverance, an erotic transformation. Any such erotic transformation involves changing not just the way we make love but also the way we live, which involves, ultimately, a transformation of society.

For many centuries, perhaps since the Pyramid Age, human life by and large has been directed toward the conquest of nature and other peoples, the exploitation of resources, the growth of central governments, the rationalization and bureaucratization of relationships, along with the glorification of what might be called the male values of competitiveness, aggressiveness, emotional armoring, and abstract thought. This approach to life has had its successes and glories, but rarely if ever has provided a climate in which erotic, transformative love could flourish. Since the birth of the nation states, in fact, the explosive creative potential of the erotic generally has been seen as a threat to the established order and has been severely constrained through both custom and law.

Today, however, there are unmistakable signs that the prevailing way of life is reaching the end of its line of development.[1] The closing of the physical frontier, the ecological, psychological, and social limitations on material growth, the specter of nuclear holocaust, and the worldwide epidemic of economic crises and anomalies all signal the end of one way of life and the dangerous, uncertain beginnings of another. Indeed, any straight-line extrapolation of present trends leads to predictions of almost certain catastrophe.

But history offers more surprises than certainties, and we would be irresponsible to rule out the possibility of a voluntary, noncatastrophic transformation of society. Such a transformation might involve a shift from competitive toward more collaborative values and behavior, from acquisitiveness toward stewardship, from glorification of aggression toward acceptance of empathy and tenderness. It might entail less centralized, less hierarchical organizational structures, with open and honest communications among individuals and groups, a systematic rather than symptomatic approach to problem solving, and a radical repersonalization of all relationships. Any benign transformation would almost certainly require that we accept a moderation in the growth rate of the advanced industrial nations, along with more material sacrifice among those at the upper than at the lower economic levels. Narrow material gain would no longer be a prime purpose of life. There would be a turn from the exploitation of physical resources to the full development of human resources, to lifelong learning, to adventures in the realms of consciousness, spirit, community, intimacy, and truly erotic love.

In this light, sexual liberation divorced from love and creation is not a revolution at all, but rather a reaction. The indiscriminate release of libido is simply the other face of sexual repression. It leads to a depersonalization and devaluation of relationships and thus of life itself, which leads in turn to the kind of despair and anomie that seeks relief in aimless travel, needless consumerism, and dependence on legal and illegal drugs. If we should ever reach the ultimate in authoritarian societies, as Huxley points out in *Brave New World*, "love," not "sex," would be a dirty word.

It is even possible to see the recent social tolerance of loveless sex as one of those desperate attempts at adaptation that have often marked the death throes of any line of cultural, biological, or artistic development: a way of keeping the masses distracted and satisfied with a consumerist, materialist society for a few more years. The outraged opposition of right-wing groups is part of the same game. A return to Victorian repressiveness would serve neither Eros nor transformation.

It is love—deeply personal, mutual, nonexploitative, erotic love—that threatens the status quo, and therefore is suspect. In our national holidays, we celebrate war and wartime leaders, "the rocket's red glare." We honor labor and dedicate the full force of seasonal consumerism to God. But love is given only a minor holiday—no parades, no banks or government offices closed. Let me propose that in a transformed society Valentine's Day would be a major holiday. If this proposal strikes you as a bit silly, then I have made my point. Our present society does not take personal, erotic love seriously, though it is precisely this love that expresses the creative force from which society itself springs.

But my purpose here is not to advocate the elevation of Valentine's Day or to promote any particular form of social transformation. It is rather to point out the connection between erotic and social, private and public, behavior. We poison the air, the water, the earth itself. Moment by moment, toxic wastes are seeping into the aquifers. A forest the size of Cuba is destroyed every year. Fertile lands are turning to dust. Species are becoming extinct at the rate of one species a day. We are partly responsible for this devastation, much of which results from our insatiable appetite for production and consumption. We trade species for annual style changes in cars and fashions, for retractable headlights, for power mowers to be used on lawns no larger than a tennis court. The species pass unmourned. The creative work of billions of years of evolution is snuffed out and not a tear is shed. We are careless. We numb ourselves. We allow ourselves to think in terms of "100 million deaths." This lack of care, this numbness, must somehow affect our lovemaking. How can we love our mates fully and without reserve so long as we have so little love for the earth?

The bedroom cannot be isolated from the rest of life. It exists at the center of an intricate web of relationships. Countless strands stretch out to the ends of the earth, and beyond. We who are hard and cold in the service of profit or ideology may seek a sanctuary of tenderness and warmth in the bedroom, but the strands of our lives still tie us to the harshness outside. In the same way, sexual inequality in the work place must eventually intrude on our most private, most erotic moments. An act of love does not exist in a vacuum. Along with our lovers' cries, there is at least a faint resonance of the cries of starving children, the percussion of violent crime, the hushed electronic hum of missile computers preset to destroy most life on this planet.

What can we do? It is better, I think, to feel the pain than to grow numb, better to acknowledge than deny the connections between the bedroom and the world. Numbness is the death of love, and we must have love, deeply felt personal love, or we will surely die. For nothing else can remedy the plague of abstraction and depersonalization that now leads us unerringly toward annihilation. The strands that connect all life carry the pain of the world into the bedroom; but if love is strong enough, there is space for sorrow and exaltation, pain and ecstasy. We love in order to feel deeply. We feel deeply in order to love. Tears and delight are the stuff of erotic surrender. To deny pain, death, and injustice is to deny love.

But we do not have to buy into injustice and depersonalization. The strands of life also reach from our private acts out into the world. By the way we make love, we influence everything else in our lives and, ultimately, our society. At best, love is not careless, but careful, full of care. It is not manipulative but mutual, not abstract but particular. It is positive, creative and unequivocally personal. Such love creates a model for a transformed society.

In this matter, Platonic love may have its own symmetry and charm, but it is not enough. For it is precisely through the responsible, passionate, fully committed joining of spirit and flesh in the act of love that we affirm our responsibility, passion, and commitment to the world.

Those who love fully, in body as well as soul, gain a special knowledge. The material world is not, as Eastern philosophers seem to suggest, an illusion. Nor is it, as Western power seekers seem to assume, an abstraction. Spirit and flesh are simply different, equal manifestations of a common vibrancy. We cannot transform one without transforming the other. The destiny of erotic love is creation—the transformation of *this* world.

Newton showed us the connection between the fall of the

apple and that of the stars. Modern physics goes farther, showing that matter and energy are one dance, that everything is relationship, that no event is totally isolated from another. We cannot escape our destiny. Our lives and our loves are not separate from the society, or from the stars. The urge that draws us together contains information about the turning of the planets, the burning of the sun. We are part of all that, and during the act of love are offered the opportunity to experience the pain and joy of creation.

In spite of a thousand failures, who would turn away from such an opportunity?

CHAPTER FIFTEEN

Creative Connections

In an age when something called "sex" is pervasive and easily available, we tend to overlook the obvious. Though erotic feelings and experience do not necessarily lead to procreation, everything in the erotic realm is, at the most fundamental level, derived from and connected to the creation of life, to creation. The creation of life, in fact, may provide us with a model for all creation. Conversely, an examination of creation in general may enrich our understanding and experience of the erotic.

The English word *creation* comes from the Latin *creare*, "to create," which is akin to the Armenian *serem*, "I bring forth." The word also has kinship with *Ceres*, the Roman goddess of growing vegetation, and *crescent*, a word that applies to the moon only when it is on the increase. In Sanskrit, *creation* bears an ancient relationship to *karma*, the destiny you create through your own actions.

The *Oxford English Dictionary* starts out by defining *creation* as "The action or process of creating; the action of bringing into existence by divine power or its equivalent; the fact of being so created." This rather tautological definition is clarified and sharpened by turning to the word *create*: "Said of the divine agent: To bring into being, cause to exist; esp. to produce where nothing was before, 'to form out of nothing'." Turning back to *creation* in the *OED*, we find a more down-to-earth account: "An original production of human intelligence or power; esp. of imagination or imaginative art."

Chinese pictograms and ideograms capture the concept of creation in a more evocative and multidimensional way. One Chinese character for *creation*, connoting "beginning," involves cutting space itself open. Another is composed of the idea of cutting from the inside outward, and then there is *creation* simply as a gate opening. A different character suggests "the mysteries": one gate opening to another gate opening to yet another all the way to the center of creation. The word shifts meaning in a lovely character involving female energy being lifted or lifting itself to a high altar to give birth.

The Chinese also have down-to-earth characters for *creation*. One is a word connected with farming and meaning "to construct or build." Another shows a knife cutting patterns in cloth. The latter character can mean "creation" or simply "a knife cutting pattern."

These definitions and symbols point us toward understanding but leave certain key questions unanswered. Is creation merely an increase of what already is: the ripening of fruit, the crescent moon growing to fullness? Or is it a novel rearrangement of existing material, as in the evolution of biological organisms or cultures or ideas? Or is something more incredible involved, an emergence of form out of chaos, even out of "nothing"?

"Increase," as in the case of burgeoning vegetation, is unquestionably one aspect of creation. But "increase" in this context is more than a mere accumulation or adding up. Creative increase involves an increase of *information*, that is to say, of meaningful relationships. A leaf is not just a linear accumulation of matter, but an arrangement of atoms, ions, molecules, and cells in highly interactive relationship. A radio is not just an accumulation of transistors, wires, coils, resistors and the like, but an arrangement—a "strategic positioning," as Benjamin Lee Whorf puts it—of these items. A concept is not just an accumulation of bits of information, but information strategically positioned and arranged in a meaningful pattern so that every bit of information can interact in some way with all the rest.

Then, too, whatever emerges from the creative process— the creative product—is in some way greater than or different from the sum of its parts. Every leaf, every ear of corn, and every living thing is unique, an entity distinct from all else in the universe. A radio, on the other hand, is not necessarily unique; to copy or mass-produce radios does not involve the creative process. But to design and build a new kind of radio is indeed creative, resulting in something unique and thus increasing the store of information in the universe. Similarly, a new concept springs from the creative process and produces an increase in information.

The same thing is true of erotic love. Every intense interpersonal relationship, and especially every intense erotic relationship, clearly creates an increase in information. *A* in relationship with *B* does not produce *AB* but rather *C*. The fictional lovers in Part I provide a case in point. Jan is an entity unique in all the universe and so is Ted. They come together and join in many ways, physical, mental, emotional, spiritual. Out of this joining is created a new entity, *Ted-and-Jan-in-relationship*, something that did not previously exist and is itself unique in the universe. The act of love described in this story produced a living being, a physical manifestation of creative increase. But physical conception is not required; the relationship itself is a new creation, increasing the richness of the universe. Whenever we fall in love, we are likely to experience a sense of wonder, surprise, and anticipation, of "a world entirely new," as one love song puts it. Perhaps this sense is no mere fancy but an intuition of an underlying truth: the creation of a new world, an opening to new possibilities.

Indeed, it is possible to see a kinship between erotic sensations and all manner of creative experience, from the creation of life to the drawing together of any significant new relationships, the emergence of any social or technical invention, the making of any work of art. Rilke tells us that "artistic experience lies so incredibly close to that of sex, to its pain and ecstasy, that the two manifestations are indeed but different forms of one and the same yearning and delight."[1] Rilke also affirms the connection between creative thought and its biological realization:

> The thought of being creator, of procreating, of 'making,' is nothing without its continuous great confirmation and realization in the world, nothing without the thousandfold concordance from things and animals—and enjoyment of it is so indescribably beautiful and rich only because it is full of inherited memories of the begetting and the bearing of millions. In one creative thought a thousand forgotten nights and love revive, filling it with sublimity and exhaltation. And those who come together in the night and are entwined in rocking delight do an earnest work and gather sweetness, gather depth and strength for the song of some coming poet, who will arise to speak of ecstasies beyond telling.[2]

Greater than the Sum of its Parts

The notion of creative increase I am putting forward here might seem to run counter to certain physical laws. According to most scientists, the physical universe is running down; that is to say, while the amount of energy it contains stays constant, the amount available for work is decreasing. Disorganization (entropy) seems to be on the rise overall. Yet there is one part of the universe—we call it "life"—which shows the opposite tendency. Living organisms capture and use ever-increasing amounts of energy. We see life forms, through the process of evolution, becoming ever more complex, more ordered, and, if you will, more beautiful. Indeed, biological evolution provides us the most compelling evidence of Eros, of the inherently creative tendency of life.

Sexual reproduction is not required for Eros to do its work. The earliest, single-celled organisms reproduced merely by splitting. Nonsexual reproduction, in fact, is more efficient in purely mechanical terms than is sexual reproduction. Great amounts of energy are used in the differentiation of two genders, as well as in the prolonged and sometimes hazardous courtship rituals of animals and humans. But sexual reproduction, whether in bacteria or human beings, makes for a rapid interchange of genetic information that immeasurably enhances and speeds up evolution. Indeed, all that we see as erotic is urgently devoted to the creation of complexity, order, and beauty, to new interconnections in the web of the world. Thus we might suspect that every attempt to trivialize this aspect of our lives is doomed to eventual failure.

To go a step further, if we look at the universe in terms of the amount of information (meaningful relationships) it holds, we might discover that it is by no means running down. According to Harvard astronomer David Layzer, "The universe is unfolding in time but not unraveling; on the contrary, it is becoming constantly more complex and richer in information." Layzer bases his formulation on the fact that in an expanding universe there is a continual increase in both entropy *and* information. This allows for the possibility that new information can be created at any time.

"The present moment always contains an element of genuine novelty," Layzer explains, "and the future is never wholly predictable. Because biological processes also generate information and because consciousness enables us to experience those processes directly, the intuitive perception of the world as unfolding in time captures one of the most deepseated properties of the universe."[3]

Creation is not something rare and strange, the exclusive

province of artists and gods. It is the plot of the universal story, the essence of our common life, the essential force behind our every desire, especially erotic desire. The universe doesn't surprise us to show off; that's the way it is. Perhaps creation resists definition primarily because it seems both ordinary and miraculous. The next chapter takes up the questions of creation from chaos and *ex nihilo* (out of nothing). For now, it is enough to say that *the creative process involves a novel rearrangement of the stuff of existence, material or nonmaterial, in which the resulting whole is in some way greater than or different from the sum of its parts. The creative product represents an increase in information.*

CHAPTER SIXTEEN

A Gift of the Night

DURING THE ACT OF LOVE, as we saw in the story of Jan and Ted in Part I, consciousness often descends through a twilight state, a sort of ecstatic chaos, in which existence seems to lose its customary form and shape. During the most powerful erotic experiences the destination of this descent involves the paradoxical apprehension of nothingness, *la petite mort*. Lovers return from such an experience renewed and sometimes transformed. It is as if, by touching chaos and the void, lovers can get in touch with something very important in existence, something involved with the creation of life itself.

So it is perhaps no accident that the most profound creation myths involve just that: creation from chaos or from nothingness. Every known human culture has some kind of narrative account of its own origins and development. Some of these creation stories are based on the idea presented in the preceding chapter: that creation merely involves a novel rearrangement of what already exists. But the most common myths evoke the mysterious creation of all things, animate and inanimate, from chaos or the void. There is an ancient resonance in these stories—of form emerging from confusion, light from darkness, of life as a gift of the night—and a strong suggestion of the connection between creation and erotic love.[1]

Form from Chaos

The chaos from which creation takes place generally is described as confusion, darkness, and water, as a substance entirely lacking in order but rich in potentiality, capable of producing all the varieties of existence. An ancient Chinese creation myth, for example, starts out as follows:

> In the beginning there was chaos. Out of it came pure light and built the sky. The heavy dimness, however, moved and formed the earth from itself. Sky and earth brought forth the ten thousand creations, the beginning, having growth and increase, and all of them take the sky and earth as their mode. The roots of Yang and Yin—the male and female principle—also began in sky and earth.
>
> Yang and Yin became mixed, the five elements separated themselves from it and a man was formed. . . .[2]

In some cases, chaos spawns a cosmic egg from which the world as we know it is born. In other cases, the cosmic egg itself contains the chaos, and the power of creativity, from which the world is formed. Even the generally more primitive Sky Father/Earth Mother myths carry the notion of potent formlessness as the precondition of creation; the primordial erotic union in these myths occurs in a state of chaos. It is only after the continually copulating world parents are separated, usually at the insistence of their offspring, that light and form emerge.

There is still another variation on the creation-from-chaos theme. In the earth-diver myths, some form of divine being, usually an animal, dives deep into water to bring up the first particles of earth from which the universe is made. Here, water represents the pregnant, unformed stuff that contains the potentiality for creation, and destruction too, for in these myths the water generally is viewed as a result of a flood that wiped out the old world in preparation for the new.

The relationship between chaos and creation is explicit in the earth-diver myths and implicit throughout the entire mythic realm. It also may be seen in primitive ceremony and ritual the world over. In the words of anthropologist Mircea Eliade, "For the archaic and traditional cultures, the symbolic return to chaos is indispensable to any new Creation."[3]

In history as well as myth, creative individuals in numerous instances have retreated to the formlessness of desert or wilderness or cave on the eve of their most creative work. Arnold Toynbee describes this phenomenon as "the pattern of withdrawal and return" and traces it out in the lives of St. Paul, St. Benedict, Gregory the Great, Buddha, Muhammad, Machiavelli, and Dante.[4]

But it is not necessary to withdraw physically in order to prepare for a creative act. Every night we withdraw into the mysterious realm of sleep and dreams, where metaphor and paradox, the essential ingredients of creation and of the erotic reign. Dreams have inspired new ideas and actions since the beginning of human history. Even in our most lucid waking moments, we are supported and driven by powerful subterranean forces, the stuff of dreams. In the process of creation and during our most powerful erotic experiences as well, we are likely to descend to this mental underworld, as the earth-diver descends into the water of chaos, to bring back to consciousness the first seeds of a new creation, a new experience of love.

Our downward progress through the caverns of the mind can be described in terms of the pulsing waves in our brains. In normal waking consciousness, the brain produces mostly beta waves of 13 to 26 cycles a second, sometimes even higher. Then, as we drop down to a relaxed, meditative mood, generally with eyes closed, our brain waves slow to the alpha state, pulsing some 8 to 13 cycles a second. Beneath this, in the twilight zone between waking and sleeping, we arrive at the theta state, with pulsations of 4 to 8 cycles a second. Brainwaves slower than 4 cycles a second, delta waves, are generally associated with sleep.

The theta state lies beneath the censorship of rational thought. It is analogous to the pregnant chaos of the creation myths, a deep cavern of the mind rich with unformed visions and unspoken words. Here we may experience the vague, often erotic yearnings and premonitions of somnambulism and sometimes become aware of "the dreamlike succession of contradictory images," in Max Ernst's words, that come one on top of the other "with the persistence and rapidity peculiar to memories of love."

Whether by coincidence or through a deep structural relationship, the theta-wave rate of pulsation matches that of musical vibrato and that of the standing wave produced in the heart-aorta system of the human body. At the top of its range, the theta-wave state also matches the electromagnetic Schumann waves that resonate at around 7.5 cycles a second all around the globe in the channel formed between the earth's surface and its ionosphere. Some theorists have speculated that Schumann waves are somehow hooked into the pulsing brain wave of those in the theta state, connecting millions of human beings at a distance and creating a sort of group consciousness. There is also some evidence that at least one hemisphere of the brain descends down through the theta state not only when in a reverie or just before sleep, but also during orgasm.[5] Perhaps, then, Borges's statement that "At the moment of orgasm, all men are one man" is not mere literary fancy.

Be that as it may, the relationship between the twilight states and creation is clear. As Brewster Ghiselin points out:

Creation begins typically with a vague, even a confused excitement, some sort of yearning, hunch or other preverbal intimation of potential resolution. Stephen Spender's expression is exact: "a dim cloud of an idea which I feel must be condensed into a shower of words."[6]

Jean Cocteau gives an example of mental withdrawal and return in the process of artistic creation:

> It would be inexact to accuse an artist of pride when he declares that his work requires somnambulism. The poet is at the disposal of his night. His role is humble, he must clean house and await its due visitation.

> The play that I am producing at the Theatre de l'OEuvre, *The Knights of the Round Table*, is a visitation of this sort. I was sick and tired of writing, when one morning, after having slept poorly, I woke with a start and witnessed, as from a seat in a theatre, three acts which brought to life an epoch and characters about which I had no documentary information and which I regarded moreover as forbidding.

> Long afterward, I succeeded in writing the play and I divined the circumstances that must have served to incite me.[7]

Entry into the caverns of reverie is not the exclusive privilege of creative genius. All of us have access to the treasures of the theta state. But the genius, unlike the person who has not harnessed his or her creative powers, withdraws into reverie from a state of highly focused commitment and passion, then returns to the tough job of making a vision into a work visible to all. In Cocteau's words, "To write, to conquer ink and paper, accumulate letters and paragraphs, divide them with periods and commas, is a different matter from carrying around the dream of a play or of a book."

Indeed, to see a vision made real—a sculptor's image of the human hand emerging from the obduracy of stone or a mathematical formula taking shape from the somnolent haze of reverie—is to witness new information entering the universe. The interplay between form and formlessness is, in any case, a key element in both the creative and the erotic processes. To sum up, *there is a strong dialectical relation-*

ship between chaos and form. The creative process is likely to entail a descent into chaos.

Creation from Nothing, the World from a Word

We have seen that creation can occur in the novel rearrangement of previously existing order and that it involves some sort of interplay with the potent formlessness of chaos. Now comes the question as to whether something can be created from nothing, and how this might relate to the experience of nothingness, the "little death" of the act of love. This paradoxical, almost unthinkable possibility is suggested in the dictionary definition of creation in many languages. It is also the theme of many creation myths. The story of creation *ex nihilo*, "out of nothing," is by no means primitive. It generally occurs in the later, more sophisticated stages of religious development, and often involves a Supreme Being, a Creator, who exists entirely outside of time and space and thus is eternal. Some of the most profound and hauntingly lovely passages in religious literature belong to this category. The *Theogony* of Hesiod for example, expresses the eighth-century B.C. Greek idea that all existence came out of the Void:

> First of all, the Void came into being, next broad-bosomed Earth, the solid and eternal home of all, and Eros, the most beautiful of the immortal gods, who in every man and every god softens the sinews and overpowers the prudent purpose of the mind. Out of Void came Darkness and black Night, and out of Night came Light and Day, her children conceived after union in love with Darkness. Earth first produced starry Sky, equal in size with herself, to cover her on all sides. Next she produced the tall mountains, the pleasant haunts of the gods, and also gave birth to the barren waters, sea with its raging surges—all this without the passion of love. Thereafter she lay with Sky and gave birth to Ocean with its deep currents. . . .[8]

The Hindu Hymn of Creation from the *Rig Veda X* is

loftier and more uncompromising in its presentation of creation *ex nihilo*:

> There was then neither non-existence nor existence;
> There was no air, no sky that is beyond it.
> What was concealed? Wherein? In whose protection?
> And was there deep unfathomable water?
>
> Death then existed not nor life immortal;
> Of neither night nor day was any token.
> By its inherent force the One breathed windless:
> No other thing than that beyond existed.
>
> Darkness there was at first by darkness hidden;
> Without distinctive marks, this all was water.
> That which, becoming, by void was covered,
> That One by force of heat came into being.
>
> Desire entered the One in the beginning;
> It was the earliest seed, of thought this product. . . .[9]

Both of these stories name erotic desire as a precondition to creation. In the Hindu version, however, desire itself is seen as a product of thought. This assumption—that all the world, all things, even time itself, spring from a thought, an idea or a statement—is common to many creation stories, including that of the book of Genesis:

> In the beginning, God created the heaven and the earth.
>
> And the darkness was without form, and void; and darkness was upon the face of the deep. And the Spirit of God moved upon the face of the water.
>
> And God said, Let there be light: and there was light.[10]

We find parallels to the Biblical creation story in cultures around the world. Before the beginning, according to the ancient Mayan creation myth, "all was in suspense, all calm, in silence, all motionless, still, and the expanse of the sky was empty." In this void, the cocreators, Tepeu and Gucumatz, meditate, discuss, and deliberate, then proceed to create the universe. The act of creation, again, consists of thoughts expressed as words:

> Thus let it be done! Let the emptiness be filled! Let the water recede and make a void, let the earth appear and become solid; let it be done. Thus they spoke. Let there be light, let there be dawn in the sky and on the earth! There shall be neither glory nor grandeur in our creation and formation until the human being is made, man is formed. So they spoke.

> Then the earth was created by them. So it was, in truth, that they created the earth. EARTH! they said, and instantly it was made.[11]

How magical this seems, how spine tingling: substance emerging from thought, the world from a word. Can we dismiss these stories as superstition or metaphor? Perhaps, but only at the risk of premature judgement. As science continues to probe the elemental mysteries, the universe, in astronomer Sir James Jeans's words, "begins to look more like a great thought than like a great machine." It is quite respectable from a scientific viewpoint to argue that information is primordial to substance or at the least that it is more efficient to describe the universe in terms of information transfer than in more conventional terms of matter and energy interactions.

The submicroscopic DNA molecule comes close to being pure information; a single strand can hold enough instructional material to fill a set of encyclopedias. And it is this information that instructs matter and energy to arrange itself into a hand, an eye, a living consciousness. At the moment of conception, DNA from two sources comes together to make a statement that we can only summarize: "Let a new human now be created out of the stuff of this world, a being that can perceive light and form, unique in all the universe, capable of further creation." And at once life begins.

As for creation out of nothing, *ex nihilo*, it must be said that our own Western scientific creation story flirts dangerously with this concept. The Big Bang Theory of creation begins with a "singularity," an inexplicable point that came into being billions of years ago and from which the entire universe expanded outward. Cosmologists speculate that the singularity might have resulted from our own universe's having pressed in on itself in a previous cycle, or perhaps as an extrusion from another universe, or just "from nothing." More precisely, the singularity presents us with an "event horizon," beyond which we can never receive information by any presently known means. In any case, wonder of wonders, a point in nothingness explodes outward to create all things, even time and space.

Say that the universe was born in this strange manner. Does that mean it was a one-time-only happening? Has all creation since then occurred merely as a construction of form out of chaos or as a rearrangement of existing order? Not necessarily. There is a way of conceptualizing creation going on all the time. As David Layzer has pointed out, truly novel information is continually being created in an expanding universe. We can look at biological evolution as one way by which the new information gets in. Cultural evolution is another. Conscious, willful creation by entities such as human beings, contributing to cultural evolution, is yet another.

Actually, it is hard to imagine that creation *ex nihilo* ended with the birth of the universe. There is more compelling symmetry in the notion that the appearance of the singularity in nothingness gives us a model of the process of creation that is still operating today. Just to behold the complexity and richness of information that has emerged through the process of biological evolution (much less the far swifter process of cultural evolution) is to gain an intuitive sense of the continuing emergence of novelty in the world. The current doctrine of evolution as the mere mechanical elimination of the unfit along with the appearance of "chance" mutations can be justified (if tortuously) through logic, but it offends our deeper knowing.

For the purposes of this exploration, in any case, let us assume that there are no completely closed systems and that there is some kind of opening in the circle of existence through which new information enters. This opening has no reliable coordinates in time and space, but is clearly marked on the map of experience. We approach it during both creative and erotic activity with vague yet powerful yearnings. We have a sense of being *on the edge*—the edge of the solution to a problem, of a religious realization, of an artistic breakthrough, of a moment of erotic passion. Here, ordinary logic dissolves and ideology yields to paradox. We fall in love. New information falls into the universe.

Creation from nothingness. Thoughts and words becoming flesh. These are strange ideas indeed. But in an age when physics and mysticism are beginning to converge, we can't easily dismiss the possibility of this mode of creation. How can I say it simply? *In some way that is beyond common understanding, creation can occur ex nihilo, out of nothing.*

Creation and Destruction

The examples of creation I have presented thus far are, to say the least, spectacular: worlds coming into being, artists and thinkers at their creative zenith. But these examples are offered only to highlight a process that is going on all the time, throughout all of nature and in every human endeavor. New species of bugs as well as of birds of paradise are still evolving. New ideas and new constructions are continually emerging in the kitchen and the factory, on the farm and on the playing field, in enterprises and adventures of every kind.

All of this involves destruction as well as construction. The creative-erotic urge that pervades society, that indeed produced the society, can also destroy it, and thus is understandably feared as well as admired. Destruction of the old is necessary for creation of the new. "Every act of creation," Picasso once remarked, "is first of all an act of destruction." Degas expressed a similar sentiment in more dramatic terms:

"A painter paints a painting with the same feeling as that with which a criminal commits a crime." Creation of the new begins with a breakdown of the old. Copernicus spent most of his creative energy trying to correct the established geocentric system. It was only after he had taken the Ptolemaic clockwork to pieces that he hit upon a way to create a new system. Marx's monumental labors in creating a new socioeconomic system were devoted as much to attacking capitalism as to formulating communism. And it is appropriate that Hegel picked the German word *Aufhebung*, with its curious double meaning of "annihilation" and "fulfillment," to describe the dialectical process of thesis, antithesis, and synthesis, which he saw as the chief mode of creation.

Both in culture and in nature, destruction serves creation. Fecundity and death are the inseparable midwives of evolution. Wherever we look in the natural world, we are confronted by the utter prodigality of life, the sacrifice of millions, billions, of individuals to create even a minor alteration in a species. Growth and decay are continually balanced and rebalanced, two aspects of a single process.

Eros, too, has its dark side. If the erotic urge can build families, it can also destroy families. The desire to join, to merge, can go over a fine line and become possession and obliteration. The most idyllic romance entails the destruction of old ties, old ways of life. And the most loving erotic act contains overtones of a primal ravishment: the rush of blood, explosions, and cries in the night. To indulge in erotic destructiveness is to become a monster. To deny the destructive element in the erotic is to make it uncreative, trivial.

Eros and the Creation of the Universe

The three modes of creation I have outlined—creation from the rearrangement of existing order, from chaos, and from nothingness—are not separate and exclusive. Most acts of creation involve not just one mode but some combination of the three. The essential point is that the whole universe as we know it is a creative process. Here the scientific creation story, our own myth, is compelling. Beginning with a singularity, a point in timelessness and placelessness, there emerged the primordial fireball, an intensely hot and energetic plasma. And out of this undifferentiated soup, through the process of time, has evolved *all this*: the spangled glory of the heavens, the immense diversity of life, the realization and potential of consciousness. The question "Why did time begin?" produces a de facto answer: "So that creation could occur."

What we often seem to forget in our desire to be sexually "free" is that Eros summons us to the ultimate creative act: the conception of a new living being. This is not to say that conception always occurs or should occur. This is not to say that erotic desire is only "valid" or "natural" when it aims at procreation; Eros, to its glory, has many manifestations. This is also not to deny that sex can become mechanical and stereotyped, which is to say noncreative. But at the heart of it, at the most fundamental level, erotic love and creation are one and the same, springing from the same source, having the same characteristics, eliciting the same ecstasy and dread.

Every erotic joining can overpass the established order, not just in that it might result in the birth of a new human individual, but in that it produces or deepens a new and powerful relationship, a single field of energy involving two previously separate individuals: something new in the existing social grouping. This joining can destroy or weaken previous bonds as well as construct new bonds, comprising novel rearrangements of the stuff of existence in which the whole is something greater than the sum of its parts.

The possibility of conception raises the stakes. The creation of a new life is, paradoxically, one of the most easily available and, simultaneously, one of the most radical of human acts. Semiconscious gropings are capable of producing another Galileo or Napoleon, an Einstein or Hitler. Every conception as well as every new erotic bond produces an increase in information. *We might say, in fact, that the feeling of erotic arousal is the anticipation of an imminent increase of information in the universe.*

In the process of erotic arousal, as well, we descend to a sort of chaos, to the potent formlessness from which new form can arise. And, ultimately, as we are drawn toward orgasm, our consciousness may take us to an ultimate night: the "event horizon," place of no place, time of no time, where paradox reigns and from which truly novel information is continually emerging into the realm of time and space.

Thus, the erotic urge summons us to creation. The act of love invites us to the terrible joys of the creative process. Caught up in fear and guilt, we often refuse the invitation. We learn not to surrender to the erotic but to use it—as a means of conquest and exploitation, as a way of measuring performance, of reducing tension. Then, when boredom inevitably overtakes us, we look for new lovers or new techniques. We seek advice from experts, sure-fire solutions to our problems.

But perhaps we achieve true liberation only when we realize that there are no sure-fire solutions. I have suggested earlier that our erotic experience is transformed not so much by what we *do* about it, what techniques we use, as by how we look at it. We can choose at any moment to see the connection between the erotic and the creative. Perceiving our erotic experience as creation rather than performance, we are freed from the quest for a mechanical reliability: the infallible arousal and orgasm, the unerring score. Instead, there is surprise and paradox; the destruction of every preconception of how "sex" is supposed to be.

CHAPTER SEVENTEEN

The Erotic Connection

SINCE STARTING WORK on this book, I have come to see myself more and more as an amateur. Against the dazzling range of erotic experience and possibility, any attempt at final authority has come to seem unjustified if not entirely futile. So if anywhere in these pages my enthusiasm has seemed to turn to prescription, I hereby cancel that prescription. If my attacks on ideology have seemed to produce another ideology, I hereby renounce that ideology. If my opinions have made the impression of universal judgements, I hereby seek to correct that impression.

In this spirit, I bring my exploration to a close by saying just what *I* want in love and sex, just in what kind of erotic world I want my children and their children to live. Please don't misunderstand: the following words are not those of a cool, objective expert but of an impassioned amateur.

Keeping the Best

I want to keep the best of the Sexual Revolution. The new freedom to talk openly about erotic matters is a blessed thing. A few straightforward words can sometimes clear up misunderstandings that would have produced a lifetime of guilt and shame in the devastating silence of times past. I want information on erotic feelings and actions, anatomy and physiology, venereal diseases and disorders, and birth control and abortion made available to people young and old in a form appropriate for their age. I believe that sympathetic, informed parents who are willing to listen as well as talk can best introduce their children to these aspects of life. The classroom, on the other hand, seems a strange place for such learning. Right now, however, with so much misinformation still around and with so many parents still unable or unwilling to deal with the subject, sex education in the schools may be a justifiable if lamentable expediency. Even so, I want it to remain purely voluntary, with no overt or covert compulsion or indoctrination. And I hope that this education would place the mechanical and medical aspects of the subject in the larger context of erotic love and creativity.

As for pornography, I don't want my children or their children or anyone else introduced to erotic activity through the sort of X-rated material I've seen. Some sex reformers argue that filmed pornography is educational and therapeutic, since it demonstrates a variety of sexual techniques and shows certain guilt-ridden individuals that they aren't the only ones in the world who practice acts they themselves consider quite idiosyncratic and perverse. This might be so, but all I've ever learned from hard-core pornography is that sex is impersonal, mechanical, devoid of any significant emotional content, and generally exploitative of women. Even if pornography is good medicine for certain adults, however, it still makes a distorted and grotesque erotic introduction for young people.

Even so, human beings are resilient, and young people are more sophisticated than we generally think. As bad as most pornography is, state censorship is, I think, even worse.

Pressing anything having to do with the erotic into a dark, forbidden corner of our society makes it not less but more dangerous. I want to live in a society that does what it reasonably can to protect children from pornography but renounces all sexual censorship for adults. I'd like to be able to see truly erotic films and read truly erotic books, in which physical joining is presented in a context of care and personal relationships, of mystery and surprise, of friendship and concern if not lasting love. Prohibition won't encourage the creation of such erotica. A transformation of erotic attitudes, starting at birth, will.

I fully support the reform of birth practices. It seems to me unfortunate, nearly tragic, that so many human beings still enter the world in harsh clinical surroundings, heavily drugged, blinded by glaring light, held upside down and slapped, and then summarily separated from their mothers. The gentler, more natural methods of child delivery and care, with the father present and involved, with the newborn infant placed immediately at the mother's breast, can set the pattern for an infancy and childhood rich in love and sensory stimulation.

The human need to be touched, caressed, cuddled, and rocked is as basic as the need for food. Babies can die of a disease called marasmus (from the Greek, "wasting away"), which is caused by lack of touch. We are now learning that sensory stimulation in infancy and childhood is necessary not only for bodily health, but also for mental development. It's becoming clear that children who are never touched lovingly may act deliberately unruly just for the sensory stimulation of a blow. Loving, nonseductive caressing of children is the ultimate sex education.

But this thing called "sex" is not separate from the rest of life. One who is caressed in childhod is more likely to caress others, to embrace the world, throughout life. One who is struck repeatedly in childhood is more likely to strike others, to savage the world, throughout life. I hate to think of the terrible acts of violence that are being committed at this moment because of lack of touch or harsh and violent touch during infancy and childhood.

Sensory and sensual pleasure, including erotic self-stimulation, is a fundamental human right. In recent decades, more and more couples have begun to exercise their freedom to try out previously forbidden erotic acts, to stimulate themselves in each other's presence, and to share erotic fantasies. To the extent that this freedom is truly free, springing from spontaneous desire rather than ideological persuasion, it can only add to the diversity and richness of all of life. Mental health, I think, is directly proportionate to the number of perceived options available to any individual. One who is mentally disturbed lives in a world in which almost every door seems closed. To close the doors of pleasure is to threaten the integrity and perhaps the sanity of the individual.

What is true of an individual is no less true of a society. I see our increasing tolerance of diverse sexual preferences as potentially a sign of social health. Heterosexual or homosexual preference, as it turns out, seems to be deeply imbedded in most people's inner being. Homosexuals and heterosexuals alike can enter into relationships that are loving, caring, creative, and responsible or those that are exploitative, depersonalized, and trivial. Each relationship must stand, not in terms of the sexual preference involved, but on its own particular qualities. I want to live in a society in which there is no bias of any type against homosexuality, bisexuality, or any other nonexploitative, nonproselytizing erotic preference.

The women's movement is, for me, the most radical and potentially most transforming movement of our times. For that reason, as well as for the sake of social justice, I support it wholeheartedly. Since the birth of civilization, the world has been precariously tipped towards the male values of aggression, competition, fragmentation, abstraction, and cold, hard logic. In a nuclear age, this imbalance is especially dangerous. We are desperately in need of nurture, feeling, intuition, wholeness, and a sense of the particular and personal. It's obviously not that men exclusively hold one set of values and women the other. It's that the general denigration of feminine values has gone along with an age-old glorification of all that is male and condescension toward all that is female. No transformation can be permanent or desirable that does not bring us back into balance.

Sexus, the ancient split between man and woman, became a chasm during the epoch of civilization. At the height of Victoria's reign, the plight of the unfeeling male, neurasthenic lady, and wretched prostitute demonstrated that in the country of "sex" everyone is an alien. There are many arguments for sexual equality, but none more compelling and immediate than the erotic. At best, making love involves a rich, complex, and powerful exchange of information: verbal, expressive, sensory, emotional, and, ultimately, moral. Its intensity lies in mutuality. In any relationship where one of the partners is treated as an inferior, the information exchange is truncated, the act of love corrupted. A meeting of unequals tends toward stereotype; standardized protocols limit the relationships of master and servant, boss and employee. A meeting of equals, however, holds nearly infinite possibilities. All changes can be rung, all games played. Roles can be switched without premeditation: now you are the more aggressive, now I. Trusting one another, we can trust the moment, whatever comes. How dull it is to "have sex" with an inferior or a superior. Erotic equality not only enriches lovemaking, but it also serves as a metaphor and a preview of sexual equality in the world at large.

Nothing Forbidden, Nothing Required

I am deeply grateful for the many new freedoms and perspectives of the Sexual Revolution. As has been clear throughout this book, however, I think we have taken some wrong turns—wherever we have split "sex" from love, creation, and the rest of life, wherever we have trivialized and depersonalized the act of love itself. These misappropriations of freedom, far more than any attacks from the so-called Moral Right, now threaten our recent gains.

Perhaps most insidious is a pervasive, covert prescription that we had better have an active and diverse sex life and that we had better start young and continue old. While working on this book, I addressed a symposium on sexuality held at a large California college. The audience of nearly a thousand was made up mostly of students. About two-thirds of the way through my talk—a fairly dry presentation of my ideas on the subject—I was startled by a loud burst of applause. What I had said was that ultimately the act of love cannot be trivialized. Afterwards, I was surrounded by a group of students. One of them, a slim, shy blonde young woman who looked no older than sixteen, thanked me with surprising fervor.

"Lately," she said, "I've been feeling guilty for not having sex on the first or second date, and I'm not getting any support from anyone for waiting for love. That's why I want to thank you for what you said."

This young women, I realized, had lived her whole life in the era of sexual liberation. In countless ways, she had absorbed one of its unspoken messages: in "sex" anything that feels good, as long as it doesn't harm someone else, is all right; nothing is forbidden. This position can be defended theoretically, but it is operationally incomplete. "Nothing forbidden" needs two more words to be even provisionally acceptable: "Nothing forbidden, nothing required."

The subtle acid of requirement curdles desire and clouds relationships. To say no when you want to say yes because you think you shouldn't is sometimes heroic. But to say yes when you want to say no because you think you should is merely grotesque. If anything in human life should be voluntary and spontaneous, erotic activity should. And yet, over the past two decades, many millions of people in the U.S. alone have forced themselves, with sinking hearts and aching guts, to try anal sex, use mechanical sex aids, or attempt multiple orgasm, to engage in premarital sex, group sex, spouse swapping, or open marriage—not because they really *wanted* to, but because they thought they *should*. I know of one couple, both psychologists, who charted their average frequency of intercourse per day to two decimal points with the express purpose of increasing it. After a few months, their chart in a tailspin, they split.

In 1968, at the full flush of the Sexual Revolution, photographer Paul Fusco and I did a lengthy feature story for *Look Magazine* on love and marriage. In the course of our research, we visited eight groups of men and women who had set up experimental living arrangements—"communes" or "extended families" in the popular terminology of the day. Four of the groups shared everything, including sexual partners. The other four shared everything except that. The sex-sharers were particularly eager to talk, to offer eloquent justifications for their positions. They told us that possessiveness, the desire to own another human being, is the greatest single obstacle to loving relationships, that jealousy is the most selfish and destructive of all emotions. True love means allowing total sexual freedom. Their experiments weren't just for themselves. They were pioneering an idea that would alleviate human suffering, contribute to the reform of society, and perhaps end war. They offered compelling examples of unselfishness and sexual joy in their own groups. We couldn't stop the torrent of words.

Indeed, if we had had to publish immediately, we would have been hard-pressed not to echo all this enthusiasm in our report, but fortunately, *Look* was willing to take its time. Six months later, just before we put the report together, Fusco and I had a chance to check back with each of the eight groups. The four that shared everything except sexual relations were still together. But the four groups of sex-sharers had all broken apart in a general atmosphere of bitterness and recrimination.

Were the spokespersons of the shattered groups now ready to admit their theories might have been wrong? Far from it. They blamed the outside culture. They offered rationalizations and excuses by the dozen. They spoke of "powerful learning experiences." But ideology held firm. The failed sharers were, in fact, more than ever convinced their theories were right, more than ever willing to talk, more than ever verbose in their advocacy.

Again and again since 1968, I have run into that same phenomenon: the sexual true believer, aflame with ideology, tireless with rationalizations. Recently, I spoke with a middle-aged woman whose husband had talked her into an open marriage. Though she had been reluctant, she was now doing everything in her power to like it. As she sought out ways to justify the experiment, her eyes darted about like those of a trapped animal. Her husband really loved her, she said; it was just that he wanted both of them to transcend possessiveness. His sexual experience with others must be seen as part of his love for her. I asked how her stomach felt about that. She said that it hurt all the time but she was working on it.

I want to be quite clear that I'm not arguing specifically against any of the erotic experiments I listed above, but only against the obligatory freedom that involves a precarious alliance of the genitals and head without the assent of the heart and guts. Dr. Wardell Pomeroy, one of the Kinsey co-authors and a leading sex authority today, told me that open marriages last an average of about two years. After that, most of the couples involved either end the experiment or end the marriage. Still (just to take open marriage as an example of experimentation), if both members really want it in their hearts and guts as well as their genitals and heads, maybe they'll find the fulfillment, however temporary, they seek. But please just do it, and spare us the rhetoric.

In the era of our liberation, the last freedom to be realized is the freedom from self-deception. For example, the Sexual Revolution of the 1960s and 1970s placed a high value on the open, honest revelation of feelings, a happy and generally beneficial reaction to the mutism of our puritanical past. But some feelings were more honored than others. Lust was honored. Anger was honored. Jealousy was not honored. Jealousy was treated as somehow unworthy of the free-swinging spirit of the times. And so we were covertly taught to discount something essential in ourselves, to ignore as best we could the pain in the belly, the ache behind the eyes.

It has taken a number of years to come around again to the obvious: jealousy can be terribly destructive, but so can its absence. Jealousy can be irrational, but so can the total lack of it. To be able to contemplate or even to watch your lover making love with another person without feeling a trace of jealousy has been called enlightenment by some revolutionaries. But this so-called enlightenment has generally turned out to involve a deadening of the heart, an abstraction of experience: the prelude to psychopathy. Jealousy is one of the form-giving passions. Its undeniable ache can help define the minimal boundaries necessary for commitment and full surrender. We can attempt to erase the boundaries through ideology and seek liberation through the total absence of form, but at some level the ache remains. And we have only to stop deceiving ourselves to realize that freedom needs form and that the total absence of boundaries constitutes the greatest tyranny.

Still, most sexologists today aim at being absolutely non-judgemental and objective about all consensual sexual activity, no matter how extreme. In view of the invidious judgements of the past, this aim can be seen as a humane one. I'm also aware that judgement and expectation are the deadly enemies of erotic surrender; at the moment of orgasm, all distinctions dissolve and there is only the pulse of the eternal present. But life goes on, and the time eventually comes for each of us to make certain decisions as to what course to pursue. It is at this point of decision that we must acknowledge that some courses are better for us than are others, that some modes of erotic activity are indeed destructive to the individual and the society. There is finally a touch of insanity in smiling blandly at sexual modes and practices that damage the physical body, that demean and debase the individual, or that further the depersonalization and trivialization of life.

The Sexual Revolution continues, but its extreme edges have become somewhat tattered and torn. The singles bars, for example, have not faded away in the mists of the sixties and seventies, but much of the glamour has gone. A man in his thirties recently told me of a brief encounter at one of those marketplaces of recreational sex. A woman who had been sitting two stools away moved over next to him and, without even a greeting, said, "I want to be totally up-front. Would you like to go back to my place and fuck?" Her invitation, which was refused on this occasion, stands as a triumph of ideology, expressing in a single stroke sexual liberation and female assertiveness.

But statements that once would have shocked now elicit yawns. Recreational sex fails eventually not because it is immoral but because it is dull. The plot can be summed up, Hollywood style, in three sentences:

Boy meets girl.
Boy gets girl.
They part.

Compared with this, even the most hackneyed boy-meets-girl story is rich with possibilities. As I pointed out earlier, the longing for story is a univeral human characteristic. The best stories, like the best games, are full of suspense, close calls, fascinating conflicts, and satisfying resolutions. The *play*, that is, the number of intense, meaningful interactions, is maximized. In this light, romance, with its yearnings, its dangers and despair, its separation and reunion, maximizes the play. A committed long-term relationship, with its difficulties, its growth, change, and sometimes heroic adaptations and transformations, maximizes the play. Recreational sex minimizes the play. It is a dreary, repetitive, boring story.

A Unique Freedom

But all the talk and the books and the films about sexual experimentation pale against the glow of truly spontaneous, deeply committed, full-bodied erotic love. For love (who can doubt it?) is a human expression of the creative force that grows great forests, that calls primeval creatures from the seas to breathe, to run, to fly. It is the force that gives life to human individuals and then joins them together into families and tribes and nations, and that must eventually unify all the world.

A few years ago, the road forked, and we travelled a few miles toward Huxley's *Brave New World*. Reading that prophetic book, we saw with terrifying clarity that wherever love is a dirty word and "sex" is compulsory, human freedom is dead. We are just now beginning to realize, I think, that wherever love is considered a nuisance, a mild embarrassment, an obstacle to "the free expression of a healthy sexuality," human freedom is endangered. We have been lost, but I believe we are finding our way again. I believe our culture can keep the best of the reform movement without giving up love and spontaneity, commitment and freedom.

Every act of love, if only we could see it afresh, is an affirmation of life, its continuation, its further evolution. Two people joining together in erotic love, as I've said more than once, create their own unique energy field, something truly original in the world. Even if procreation is neither the result nor the purpose, their joining is still an act of creation. The news beams out to all the universe. There has been an increase in information, in complexity, in form. Somewhere in the vast dark sea of entropy, there is a new energy, a new glow. An entity is born! No wonder lovers want to bear witness to their love, to shout it from the highest hill. What is most ordinary is most extraordinary. Love is the News without which there can be no news, no perception, no life.

For me, the erotic encounter is ecstatic in the dictionary sense of the word. It takes me out of my set position, my stasis. It permits me the unique freedom of stripping away every mask, every facade that I usually present to the world, and of existing for a while in that state of pure being where there is no expectation and no judgement. The act of love, at best, is an unveiling. Layer after layer of custom and appearance are stripped away. First goes clothing, then every other marker of status and position: job, title, honors, monetary worth. Propriety must also go, and with it pride. My freedom lies precisely in surrender, in my willingness to relinquish even my hard-won personality (*persona*, Greek for "mask"), my image of who I am in the world and what I should be—my ego. If I am willing to travel this far and expect nothing, then nothing can go wrong. There are no "sexual problems," no "sexual solutions." There is no technique. I am as a god; whatever happens happens.

And it is in this state of surrender, of not-trying, that my full erotic potential is realized. For I am now willing to lose everything and find nothing. All that has maintained me in the ordinary world is of no use here—grammar, syntax, sensory acuity. Even differences of gender fade away in the climactic rhythm of our joining. I am not male, my love is not female. We are one, one entity. Through the tumult of love, we have arrived at a radiant stillness, the center of the dance.

At this point, there is a choice that lies beyond conscious choice, predisposed by trust, commitment and passion: to travel even beyond space and time and enter a sublime darkness. Seeing nothing, hearing nothing, I am totally connected with my love, and, through her, to all of existence. What was veiled is unveiled, what was hidden is revealed;

beneath all appearance, beyond all customary distinctions, there is a deeper self that wears no mask. In the darkness, there is an illumination. In love, I have found nothing and all things.

It's not always like that. If erotic love is extraordinary, it is also commonplace. There are occasions when the act of love simply soothes and nurtures. There are times when a caring lover, half-asleep, may simply lend his or her body to a more aroused partner as a gesture of friendly love. There are also episodes of pure genital lust, exuberant carnal joy. Not everyone can find a lifelong, committed erotic relationship, but everyone can be caring rather than mechanical, giving rather than manipulative. Love has many names and many faces and is not in short supply. Every erotic act offers the possibility of a loving human interaction. To deny or fail to appreciate the commonplace is to reduce the possibility of transcending it. I have also learned over the years that living organisms are not machines, that erotic arousal is not a predictable, mechanical phenomenon. Love is like the weather: unpredictably cyclical. A sudden, unforeseen fall of desire doesn't necessarily mean rejection or the end of a relationship. It is probably only a change in the weather of love. To try to force arousal during a dry spell or to give up and seek "sex" elsewhere is to shut out the cloudburst of passion that in all likelihood will follow (though no one can say just when). To wait patiently, to ride lightly with the rhythms of life, is no failure of will or action. For even during a lull of physical passion, the light of our joining is in my lover's eyes. Under every conceivable sky, we remain connected—to one another and to all things.

That erotic connection will hold me to my lover and to life for as long as I live. I will seek responsibility because joining my body with hers is the ultimate responsibility. I will be trusting because trust is the other side of surrender, and the deeper connection is impossible without surrender. I will commit myself to her without demanding possession be-cause the mere thought of owning her makes her an object, an *It*. I will open myself to the unpredictable, the mysterious, sensing a sort of poetic physics of love. In the quantum world, the more we know about the position of an elementary particle, the less we know about its momentum. In love, I think, the more we try to pin a lover down, the less momentum, the less movement and excitement, we experience. I will not try to pin my lover down. Danger, uncertainty and a touch of the forbidden add to the thrill of our every moment together. In all the primates, including humans, the presence of a sexual rival increases the flow of sex hormones. But I need no contrived danger. No rival for her love is required to increase my excitement. For I know that death is my inexorable rival. Sooner or later death will separate us. In this realm of being, we must say goodbye. Perhaps more than anything else, our full awareness of death's capriciousness and inevitability makes our love both poignant and profound.

It is the glory and grace of erotic love that it offers each of us the opportunity of passionate connection with another and, through that, of a larger connectedness. The erotic urge draws us toward creation, toward the condition of potent nothingness from which all existence unfolds. To make love is ultimately to affirm life, new families, new generations. In the light of truly personal erotic love, war is no longer abstract, a matter of cold statistics ("only 100 million deaths"), but rather a matter of immediate personal concern. The possible destruction of life on earth is no longer *out there* but here, in this place and this time: the possible destruction of our love, of all love.

I believe that erotic love can serve as a healing force in a dangerous world. It shatters any ideology that fails to distinguish lives from ideas. It leads us to experiences in which it is not necessary to take a drug, commit a crime, or go to war in order to feel fully awake and alive. It connects us to other people and to all the earth and perhaps to the stars as well.

And if erotic love is too important to be repressed, it is

also too important to be devalued, for to devalue love is to devalue life itself. I want my children and their children to live in a world in which the depersonalization and trivialization of the erotic is no longer rationalized and glorified. I would like someday soon to celebrate the end of "sex" and the beginnings of a radically repersonalized, fully erotic society.

Our current situation is perilous. As always, the game is a close one. But I believe—in some way we must all believe—that love will prevail, that love eventually will join us in a family as wide as all humankind that can laugh together, weep together and share the common ecstasy.

Notes

Introduction

1. See Daniel Yankelovich, "New Rules in American Life: Searching for Self-Fulfillment in a World Turned Upside Down," *Psychology Today*, April 1981, p. 39.

2. See *Sexuality Today* 4, no. 35 (June 22, 1981): 1–2.

3. Shere Hite, *The Hite Report* (New York: Dell, 1977), p. 588.

Chapter 1

1. Alfred C. Kinsey, Wardell B. Pomeroy, Clyde E. Martin, and Paul H. Gebhart, *Sexual Behavior in the Human Female* (Philadelphia and London: W. B. Saunders, 1953), pp. 604–605.

2. Ibid., p. 606.

3. Ibid., p. 613.

Chapter 2

1. I am especially indebted to Masters and Johnson for their pioneering research on the sexual response sequence. See William H. Masters and Virginia E. Johnson, *Human Sexual Response* (Boston: Little, Brown and Co., 1966).

Chapter 6

1. *Hesiod's Theogony*, trans. Norman O. Brown (New York: The Liberal Press, 1953), p. 56.

2. Sigmund Freud, *Civilization and Its Discontents*, trans. James Strachey (New York: W. W. Norton, 1962), p. 69.

Chapter 7

1. Erwin J. Haeberle, *The Sex Atlas* (New York: The Seabury Press, 1978).
2. Rev. Ted McIlvenna, Ph.D., and Rev. Laird Sutton, Ph.D., *Meditations on the Gift of Sexuality* (San Francisco: Specific Press, 1977).
3. Haeberle, op. cit., p. 487.

Chapter 8

1. See Elman R. Service, *The Hunters* (New York: Prentice-Hall, 1966), pp. 83–84.
2. Michael Foucault, *The History of Sexuality*, vol. I (New York: Pantheon Books, 1978), p. 33.
3. Thomas Berger, *Little Big Man* (New York: Fawcett, 1964), pp. 213–214.
4. *The Iliad of Homer*, trans. by Andrew Lang, Walter Leaf, and Ernest Myers (New York: The Modern Library, 1950), p. 435.
5. Joseph Campbell, *The Masks of God: Creative Mythology* (New York: Viking Press, 1976), p. 53.
6. Ibid., pp. 42–83.

Chapter 9

1. Bernie Zilbergeld, *Male Sexuality* (New York: Bantam Books, 1978), p. 23.
2. Harold Robbins, *The Betsy* (New York: Pocket Books, 1971), pp. 101–103, quoted in Zilbergeld, pp. 25–26.
3. Norman Mailer, *Advertisements for Myself* (New York: Signet Books, 1960), p. 424.
4. Ibid., p. 450.
5. Anaïs Nin, *Delta of Venus* (New York: Bantam, 1978), pp. xiii–xiv.
6. Ibid., pp. 95–96.

Chapter 10

1. Thomas Hobbes, *Leviathan*, trans. C. B. Macpherson (Baltimore: Pelican Books, 1968), p. 161. (First published in 1651.)
2. Ibid., p. 186.
3. Sigmund Freud, *Civilization and Its Discontents*, ed. James Strachey (New York: Norton, 1961), p. 58.

4. Quoted in Arthur M. Wilson, *Diderot* (New York: Oxford University Press, 1972), p. 380.

5. Quincy Wright, *A Study of War*, 2d ed. (Chicago: University of Chicago Press, 1965), p. 39.

6. See Erich Fromm, *The Anatomy of Human Destructiveness* (New York: Fawcett, 1973); see also Abraham Maslow, *Toward a Psychology of Being* (New York: Viking Press, 1968); Carl Rogers, *On Becoming a Person* (Boston: Houghton Mifflin, 1961); also Chapter Five of my book, *The Transformation* (Los Angeles: J. P. Tarcher, 1981).

7. Martin Buber, *I and Thou*, 2d ed. (New York: Scribner, 1958), p. 34.

8. William J. Lederer and Don D. Jackson, M.D., *The Mirages of Marriage* (New York: W. W. Norton, 1968), p. 130.

Chapter 11

1. James W. Prescott, "Body Pleasure and the Origins of Violence," *The Futurist*, April 1975, pp. 64–74.

2. See Wilhelm Reich, *Character Analysis*, trans. Theodore P. Wolfe, 3rd, enlarged edition (New York: Noonday Press, 1965).

3. See Daniel Yankelovitch, *New Rules* (New York: Random House, 1981); and Louis Harris, "Our Changing Structure of Values," in Sheppard and Carroll, eds., *Working in the 21st Century* (New York: John Wiley and Sons, 1980).

Chapter 12

1. Dr. Manfred Clynes, *Sentics: The Touch of Emotions* (Garden City: Anchor Press/Doubleday, 1977).

2. See Bernard d'Espagnat, "The Quantum Theory and Reality," *Scientific American*, November 1979, pp. 158–181.

3. For a fuller discussion of holonomy and also of human uniqueness, see my book, *The Silent Pulse* (New York: Dutton, 1978), especially pp. 48–106.

4. Nathaniel Branden, *The Psychology of Romantic Love* (Los Angeles: J. P. Tarcher, 1980), pp. 117–118.

5. Carl Rogers, *Becoming Partners* (New York: Delacorte Press, 1972).

6. Simone de Beauvoir, *The Second Sex*, trans. H. M. Parshley (New York: Knopf, 1961), p. 420.

7. George B. Leonard, *The Man & Woman Thing* (New York: Delacorte Press, 1970), pp. 157–158.

Chapter 13

1. For a concise, comprehensible description of Prigogene's theory and its significance for personal and social transformation, see Marilyn Ferguson, *The Aquarian Conspiracy* (Los Angeles: J. P. Tarcher, 1980), pp. 162–170.

2. Betty Grayson and Morris I. Stein, "Attracting Assault: Victims' Nonverbal Cues," *Journal of Communications* 31, no. 1, Winter, 1981, pp. 68–75.

3. Northrop Frye, *Fearful Symmetry* (Princeton: Princeton University Press, 1947), p. 431.

4. Norman O. Brown, *Love's Body* (New York: Vantage, 1966), pp. 126–140.

5. Alfred North Whitehead, *Process and Reality* (New York: Harper Torchbooks, 1929), p. 184.

6. Joseph Bedier, *The Romance of Tristan and Iseult*, trans. Hilaire Belloc and Paul Rosenfeld (New York: Doubleday Anchor, 1953), pp. 47–48.

Chapter 14

1. Numerous books and studies support the thesis of inevitable social transformation. Among them, see my book, *The Transformation* (Los Angeles: J. P. Tarcher, 1981); Jonas Salk, *The Survival of the Wisest* (New York: Harper & Row, 1973); Donella H. Meadows and others, *The Limits of Growth: A Report for the Club of Rome's Project on the Predicament of Mankind* (New York: Universe Books, 1972); Marilyn Ferguson, *The Aquarian Conspiracy* (Los Angeles: J. P. Tarcher, 1980); Theodore Roszak, *Person/Planet* (Garden City, N.Y.: Anchor Press/Doubleday, 1978); Jeremy Rifkin, *Entropy: A New World View* (New York: Viking, 1980); and *The Global 2000 Report to the President: Entering the Twenty-First Century* (U.S. Government Printing Office, 1981).

Chapter 15

1. Quoted in John J. L. Mood, *Rilke on Love and Other Difficulties* (New York: W. W. Norton, 1975), p. 36.

2. Ibid., pp. 34–35.

3. Quotations from David Layzer, "The Arrow of Time," *Scientific American*, December 1975, pp. 56–59.

Chapter 16

1. An excellent guide to creation stories is found in Charles H.

Long, *Alpha: The Myths of Creation* (New York: G. Braziller, 1963).

2. Claus W. Krieg, *Chinesische Mythen Und Legenden* (Zurich, 1946), pp. 7–8; quoted in Ibid., p. 126.

3. Mircea Eliade, *Myths, Dreams and Mysteries*, trans. Philip Mairet (New York: Harper Torchbooks, 1967), p. 80.

4. Arnold Toynbee, *A Study of History*, abridged by D. C. Somervell (New York: Oxford University Press, 1947), pp. 217–230.

5. Harvey D. Cohen, Raymond C. Rosen, and Leonide Goldstein, "Electroencephalographic Laterality Changes During Human Sexual Orgasm," *Archives of Sexual Behavior* 5, no. 3, 1976, pp. 189–199.

6. Brewster Ghiselin, *The Creative Process* (New York: New American Library, 1955), p. 14.

7. Ibid., p. 82.

8. *Hesiod's Theogony*, trans. Norman O. Brown (New York: The Liberal Arts Press, 1953), p. 56.

9. S. Radhadrishnan and C. A. Moore, eds., *A Source Book on Indian Philosophy* (Princeton: Princeton University Press, 1957), p. 24.

10. *The Holy Bible*, Authorized King James Version (London and New York: Oxford University Press, 1945), p. 7.

11. Adrian Recinos, *Popol Vuh: The Sacred Book of the Ancient Quiche Maya*, trans. Delia Goetz and Sylvanua G. Morley (Norman, Oklahoma: University of Oklahoma Press, 1950), p. 81.

Index

ABOUT THE AUTHOR

GEORGE LEONARD is the author of the best sellers *Education and Ecstasy*, *The Transformation*, *The Ultimate Athlete*, and *The Silent Pulse*. He was senior editor at *Look* for seventeen years and is past president of the Association for Humanistic Psychology.